Endorsements for *Eat Like a Heroine*

"*Eat Like a Heroine* draws timeless culinary wisdom from classic literature to inspire us to dine well every day. A complete joy to read. I give it a chef's kiss!"

> – **Jennifer L. Scott,** New York Times bestselling author of
> *Lessons from Madame Chic*

"You are holding a joyful book in your hands! If you chose this book, you're probably a lot like me. I grew up reading the classics, and I immersed myself in the lives of the heroines within each book as I read. I can still envision the way *The Secret Garden* was mapped out in my head, or how it felt to live in the attic of *The Little Princess*. I roamed the prairie with Laura Ingalls and her family, and the Alps with Heidi.

I don't remember any of the heroines going on a diet, counting calories, or fretting about the macros they were eating. Food was part of every celebration. Then I grew up.

Enter diet culture. Eating suddenly became difficult, because of the messages we received all around us. I struggled with my weight for years, until I embraced living an intermittent fasting lifestyle in 2014. By doing so, I was finally able to lose 80 pounds and change my relationship with both food and my body. I eat with joy each day, like a heroine. I celebrate holidays with my family and friends, and the celebrations all include food that is meant to be shared and enjoyed. I have rediscovered my love of cooking, and it is one of my daily pleasures in life to create a beautiful meal for my family.

So, take a trip down memory lane as you read about the heroines in this book, and discard modern diet culture in favor of a rediscovered love of food and eating, and celebrating with those you love."

> – **Gin Stephens,** author of NY Times Bestseller *Fast. Feast.*
> *Repeat.* and host of two podcasts: Intermittent Fasting Stories
> and Fast Feast Repeat Intermittent Fasting for Life

" A fanciful combination of literary history, cookbook, and how-to guide, *Eat Like a Heroine* reintroduced me to the spunky characters and writers I fell in love with in childhood, then combined them with my favorite pastime: eating! Lorilee and Jenny reminded me there are so many ways to be a heroine in my own life and in the lives of the people I love. I can't wait to share this book with my fellow readers!"

— **Annie B. Jones,** author and owner of The Bookshelf

" This book is a lovely melting pot of goodness for bookish friends and foodies alike! And the 'SECRET' ingredients for this dish are Lorilee and Jenny, who bring a dash of delight, a cup of curiosity, and an extra pinch of personality and passion to its pages. Buy it for yourself to taste and see!"

— **Keri Wilt,** head & heart cultivator over at The Well-Tended Life, a mission inspired by the words of her Great-Great-Grandmother, Frances Hodgson Burnett, author of *The Secret Garden.*

Eat Like a Heroine

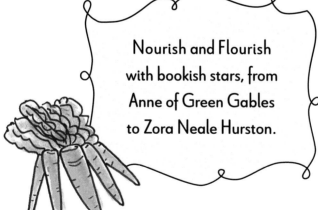

Nourish and Flourish
with bookish stars, from
Anne of Green Gables
to Zora Neale Hurston.

LORILEE CRAKER *and* JENNY WILLIAMS

Dedication

For my very own A-Z, my two nieces, Amanda McHugh and Zoe Reimer.
I have cherished watching you both grow into the heroines
I always knew you were. I love you both forever.
–Lorilee

For my mom, Debbie Clem: the heroine who taught me the most
about cooking and hospitality, and who let me read past my bedtime.
With love and gratitude.
And for Grandma Fern: I can't wait to discuss Jane Eyre with you.
–Jenny

Eat Like a Heroine: Nourish and Flourish with Bookish Stars
from Anne of Green Gables to Zora Neale Hurston
Copyright © 2024 by Lorilee Craker and Jenny Williams. All rights reserved.

End Game Press books may be purchased in bulk at special discounts for sales promotion, corporate gifts, ministry, fund-raising, or educational purposes. Special editions can also be created to specifications. For details, contact Special Sales Dept., End Game Press, P.O. Box 206, Nesbit, MS 38651 or info@endgamepress.com.
Visit our website at www.endgamepress.com.
Library of Congress Control Number: 2024936809
ISBN: 978-1-63797-136-9
eBook ISBN: 978-1-63797-225-0
"The Bean Eaters" Reprinted By Consent of Brooks Permissions.
Cover and interior art by Jenny Williams
Design by Monica Thomas for TLC Book Design, *TLCBookDesign.com*
Published in association with Don Pape of Pape Commons

Printed in India

10 9 8 7 6 5 4 3 2 1

Dear Heroine,
YOU are CORDIALLY
INVITED to join
us around THE
(METAPHORICAL) table—
for a FEAST for
THE SOUL—where
kindred spirits
GATHER—AND THERE
is ROOM FOR
everyone.
LC + JW ♡

CONTENTS

INTRODUCTION 9

CHAPTER 1 PICNIC LIKE A HEROINE 15
RECIPE JENNY'S FETA PASTA SALAD 29

CHAPTER 2 COMFORT LIKE A HEROINE 33
RECIPE CASSIE LOGAN'S CROWDER PEAS 47

CHAPTER 3 OFFER PINAFORE HOSPITALITY
LIKE A HEROINE 49
RECIPE JENNY'S FAVORITE LAST-MINUTE
DUTCH BABY PANCAKE 62

CHAPTER 4 PROFFER PUFFED SLEEVE HOSPITALITY
LIKE A HEROINE 65
RECIPE LORILEE'S CRAZY EASY, BUDGET-FRIENDLY,
FANCY SLOW COOKER RED WINE-SOAKED
PEARS 81

CHAPTER 5 COZY LIKE A HEROINE 85
RECIPE MAYA ANGELOU'S BUTTERMILK BISCUITS 99

CHAPTER 6   NOURISH LIKE A HEROINE 101

RECIPE   NOURISHING & DELICIOUS CHICKEN
POT PIE SOUP 118

CHAPTER 7   EAT LOCAL LIKE A HEROINE 121

RECIPE   LORILEE'S BEST & EASIEST VENISON
RECIPE EVER 135

CHAPTER 8   HOLIDAY LIKE A HEROINE 137

RECIPE   LOUISA MAY ALCOTT'S APPLE SLUMP ... 152

CHAPTER 9   OBSESS LIKE A HEROINE 155

RECIPE   MARZIPAN HEDGEHOG 168

CHAPTER 10   BOND WITH YOUR HERITAGE
LIKE A HEROINE 171

RECIPE   LORILEE'S MENNONITE WHITE SAUCE ... 186

RECIPE   GRANDMA FERN'S SOUR CREAM SOFTIES .. 187

CHAPTER 11   REDEEM FOOD SCRAPES & DISASTERS
LIKE A HEROINE 191

RECIPE   MRS. BARRY'S HUMBLE PIE 204

ACKNOWLEDGMENTS 207

ENDNOTES 211

EXPERIENCE YOUR
favorite books,
CHARACTERS,
and authors, IN
AN ENTIRELY new
and RELISHABLE way.

INTRODUCTION

WHY SHOULD WE EAT LIKE OUR FAVORITE BOOK HEROINES AND CLASSIC AUTHORS?

Turns out, our beloved book characters from *Anne of Green Gables* to the most cherished classic authors such as Zora Neale Hurston can teach us everything about improving the quality of our lives through the food we cook, eat, serve, and share with others. In these pages, join us—two kindred spirits—as we travel through the classic novels we love, gleaning the most golden foodie wisdom on picnicking, comfort, compassion, hospitality, coziness—nourishing and flourishing. Each chapter addresses an of-the-moment problem and offers timeless and savvy heroine solutions for a more openhearted, compassionate, and well-nourished life. Every chapter will feature one heroine leading the way—say Maya Angelou or one of *Little Women's* March sisters—and folds in a curated blend of the best advice on that particular foodie topic from an array of bookish stars.

THE HEROINES WERE FOODIES, NO DOUBT ABOUT IT

We present as exhibit A, Emily Dickinson, who wrote poems on the backs of recipes, and recipes on the backs of poems. It's almost as if poetry was her Side A, and cooking was her Side B.

In her mid-twenties, once sociable Emily began to shrink back from human company outside her home. Her anxiety deepened, though cooking and baking in the kitchen with her beloved Irish maid, Maggie, comforted her and gave her another outlet beyond poetry. A recluse by then, she still loved to share her treats with others. Emily sent bountiful boxes of her chocolate caramels and other cakes to friends and family members, with the recipes tucked inside. Famously, she hid behind the drapes of an upper story room, and lowered baskets of gingerbread and cream puffs to neighborhood children lurking below. This picture, of dear Emily sharing her food with others so winsomely, despite her mental health struggles, pierces our hearts and makes us love her forevermore.

Two years before Emily's death, she wrote her cousins about baking a "loaf cake" with Maggie in the kitchen when "I saw a great darkness coming and knew no more until late at night." Sadly, after this collapse, Emily was never well again. But food—watching it grow, harvesting it, baking it, and cooking it—sustained her in more ways than one.

Food also shaped other heroines and authors. We think of our A-Z–*Anne of Green Gables* to Zora Neale Hurston. Anne's author, Lucy Maud Montgomery, was a wonderful cook who also whisked into her books many references to eating, menus, secret recipes (we're looking at you, Old Lady Pringle, with your hush-hush pound cake recipe, calling for thirty-six eggs!), and most prominently, kitchen catastrophes, or "scrapes" as she called them. We don't think we would love Anne half so much had she not accidentally drowned a mouse in the plum pudding sauce, or inadvertently flavored a layer cake with liquid pain reliever instead of vanilla.

And Zora? She was a cook, an eater, an anthropologist, and a writer who relished all things food related. In her most famous work, *Their Eyes Were Watching God*, the 1937 novel on Black Southern womanhood, people eat soda crackers with cheese, sip lemonade, or freshen their water with ribbon cane syrup, and serve whole barbecued hogs with sweet-potato pone. A man who is feeling flush offers fried chicken and macaroni for all, and Janie, the heroine, leaves her loveless first marriage, but not before frying her old husband a hoecake to go with his coffee.

The more we stirred the pot, so to speak, the more we discovered that our most beloved authors didn't just season their writing with food-related scenes, they were quite obsessed on a personal level. Maya Angelou, who, along with Laura Ingalls Wilder, wrote sumptuously about food before food writing was a thing, owned more than three hundred cookbooks and wrote two of her own. Someone once said that she was an even better cook than she was a writer!

Wilder, who included thirty pages on maple syrup and nine pages on cheese alone in her first book, *Little House in the Big Woods*, tucked her recipe for gingerbread in letters responding to fan mail. Laura's gingerbread has become the feature of thousands of celebrations held in her honor all over the world.

Jane Austen, however, may win the prize: the first recorded use of the word "sponge-cake" is by Jane, as verified in the *Oxford English Dictionary*. Writing to her sister Cassandra in 1808, Jane wrote, "You know how interesting the purchase of sponge-cake is to me." Perhaps she even watched or participated in the making of an early iteration, as Jane lived for years with her dear friend, housekeeper, and subsequent sister-in-law, Martha Lloyd, the author of a compendium of recipes and remedies called *Martha Lloyd's Household Book*. Martha's epicurean influence definitely sifted into her housemate's novels, and we can't wait to introduce you to Jane the Foodie.

Actually, we are thrilled to introduce you to the "savorer side" of all our favorite heroines, which in this case, refers to not just fictional characters, but the women writers who created those characters, and inspire us still with their words and lives.

ELEVEN ELEVATIONS

In these pages, we explore eleven ways the heroines teach us how to elevate our eating and cooking lives, including how we can boost the way we offer hospitality, celebrate holidays, eat locally and seasonally, and redeem our most embarrassing food-related moments.

There's just so much to relish when it comes to books and food, and food in books! You already adore these classics, modern and vintage, returning to them again and again for delight, comfort, and companionship. Now you can experience your favorite books, characters, and authors in an entirely new and relishable way.

So why should we eat like a heroine? In short, we humbly suggest that eating like a heroine will assist each of us in our own journeys of character growth and transformation. A way of eating that is nourishing to both body and soul? In the quasi-words of our girl Jane Austen, "Is this not pleasant?"

We hope you'll agree that, yes, it really is!

List your favorite heroines

....
....
....
....
....
....
....
....
....
....
....
....
....
....
....
....
....
....
....
....

"In an INCREDIBLY SHORT time EVERY vestige OF THE pie HAD DISAPPEARED, and a blissful STICKINESS PERVADED the PARTY."

— WHAT KATY DID

Chapter 1

PiCNiC LiKE A HEROiNE

Achieve "Blissful Stickiness" like Katy Carr

> "There's something dreamy about eating like an old-world aristocrat."
>
> REVELRY PICNICS

PROBLEM: You think of picnics as drab and joyless affairs. You may think picnicking is for other people, not you.

HEROINE SOLUTION: Eating outside on the ground is the lost art our grownup social lives are missing: it's playful, far less intimidating than a dinner party, and allows us to see our friends (and dare we say, the world?) in an entirely different light. Thankfully, our heroines teach us how to REVEL joyfully in picnics, from modest and simple to more elaborate.

*N*O ONE PICNICS as blissfully as a heroine, from Maya Angelou, raving about a scandalously secret barbeque sauce to Anne of Green Gables rhapsodizing over her first taste of ice cream at the upcoming Sunday School soiree.

Our heroines knew the secrets to superior al fresco dining: inspiring outdoor locales, surprising treats, and, in Emma Woodhouse's case, learning when to keep one's trap shut. (What she said to Miss Bates at the Box Hill Picnic? We're with Mr. Knightly on this: Badly done, Emma. Although, in her defense, she did just nosh on cold pigeon pie, so perhaps she was about to "upswallow," as the British say, one of their many fine euphemisms for throwing up.) Or maybe Emma was just being a bit mean, as she was wont to do before her transformation. But then again, every heroine is so much more than her worst moment, and this *was* Emma's worst moment.

So we don't look to Emma for picnicking advice; she is not exactly a leading light in the moveable feast department. Not to mention, she had a squad of servants doing all the work, and picnicking can be a bit of work.

Other literary luminaries, though, picnicked with flamboyance, brio, and joy. We'd love to taste that indecent sauce with Maya, and witness Anne take her first lick of ice cream. But neither of those heroines is the one we'd most like to pack a basket with. That heroine is Katy Carr, of *What Katy Did* fame. What *she* did was picnic like a boss. This lady knew what she was doing in terms of elevating the plowman's lunch to something magical, something fairylike.

It must be said: Aunt Izzie, Katie's crabby maiden aunt, was basically the Fairy Foodmother in this piece. It was she who anticipated the appetites of her nieces and nephews and their posse, and she who filled not one but two baskets with a bounty:

"First came a great many ginger cakes. These were carefully laid on the grass to keep till wanted; buttered biscuit came next—three apiece, with slices of cold lamb laid in between; and last of all were a dozen hard-boiled eggs, and a layer of thick bread and butter sandwiched with cold beef."

Two kinds of sandwiches, then, and a dozen hard boiled eggs. Sounds hearty and satisfying. For all her unfortunate qualities, Aunt Izzie was a feeder extraordinaire. But a picnic is so much more than just lunch on a blanket. A picnic feeds the spirit as much or more than the body.

Katy knew that a big part of the magic was the "where" of the picnic. She and her troupe tramped a short distance on their property, through the woods to a grassy knoll shaded by poplar trees. Here they went the extra step and built a "bower of boughs hung over skipping ropes" and "they all cuddled underneath." Oh, the sweetness! Katy, her sister Clover, and best friend Cecy, plus some little siblings, crafted a hideaway for themselves as they feasted on Aunt Izzie's sandwiches. The birds sang, the wind whirled in the trees, and the woods smelled fresh and green. "No grown-up dinner party ever had half so much fun." Seriously. You can feel the wistfulness in author Susan Coolidge's description. By the time she wrote *Katy* in 1872, she was thirty-six and had no doubt endured any number of stodgy, dodgy, grownup dinner parties. She based Katy on herself and her own lucky childhood with four siblings in Cleveland, Ohio, which makes her fetching novel even more poignant.

Ah, picnics. They charm us because they take us back to our childhood days of freedom and leisure, when even mushy egg salad sandwiches tasted great at the park. And the shimmer of picnics becomes downright sparkly when you add a surprise, something you wouldn't eat on an ordinary day. Writer Kate Hill, in a *Saveur* article called "How to Picnic Like the French," tips us off to her secrets for the most effervescent outdoor dining.

"I fill my picnic baskets, sometimes full of antique linens and silver, sometimes paper plates and beach towels, and always something delicious. The end result should be like the best Christmas presents, where more and more surprising treats are disclosed…"

A picnic could be ordinary in every way but when the pop (or pops) of wonder is revealed, things go from flat to fizzy in a snap.

At Katy's picnic, this is where the second basket came into play. Yes, the second basket! Lamb sandwiches on biscuits are all well and good, but when the last crumb disappeared, Katy knew her moment had come: she produced another basket and lifted the lid.

"Oh, delightful surprise!" Aunt Izzie—perhaps not such a crank after all—had tucked seven little molasses pies inside for dessert. Coolidge, who missed her calling as a food blogger, goes to town as she describes these alluring small bites. "Molasses pies, baked in saucers—and each with a brown top and crisp, candied edge, which tasted like toffee and lemon peel and all sorts of good things mixed together."

Katy and the other picnic goers began exulting in a "general shout" and all were overcome by a "tumult of joy." In other words, there was a hullabaloo of happiness, inspired by not just the picnic itself, but by the reveal of a small indulgence for each picnic goer at the end. The cherry on top of the sundae. The crux of the biscuit. A little gravy, baby! You get it. It's that final flourish that makes a picnic special.

Special, and sticky, at least for Katy and company. Mere seconds after they demolished Aunt Izzy's mini molasses pies, every crumb of pie had vanished, and—we adore this line—"a blissful stickiness pervaded the party."

A "blissful stickiness," huh? We take this to mean joyfully messy, an exuberant state of being, a heavenly jumble of tactile, uninhibited pleasures of good food and fresh air. When you're so elated and carefree, you don't even care about the gummy molasses on your hands, or the tacky barbeque sauce on your cheeks, you know you're having the best, most carefree time.

We have a feeling that the picnic Maya Angelou describes in *I Know Why the Caged Bird Sings* lived up to the high bar set by "blissful stickiness":

"The summer picnic gave ladies a chance to show off their baking hands. On the barbecue pit, chickens and spareribs sputtered in their own fat and a sauce whose recipe was guarded in the family like a scandalous affair."

Now that is a secret sauce! We would give a lot for that hush-hush recipe. Did it have ketchup, brown sugar, Worcestershire sauce, lemons, and cider vinegar? Or garlic, paprika, Tabasco sauce, and butter? Maybe Miss Maya was never able to lay hands on the recipe, shielded as it was from outsider eyes like a deep, dark secret. Even though Maya was a famously good cook and even wrote two cookbooks, we can't find a recipe for barbeque sauce. The closest is a recipe for baked beans, featuring molasses, sugar, and dried mustard.

Maybe the secret sauce did have molasses in it—there have been, after all, countless saucepans bubbling with a sweet, spicy, sticky molasses-based sauce. Molasses mini pies or molasses barbeque sauce—either way, blissful stickiness was achieved at Katy's picnic and Maya's, too.

"Do the best you can until you know better," Maya said once. "Then when you know better, do better." Now that we know better, now that we know about Blissful Stickiness, we want our future fresh air meals to attain higher levels of stickiness and blissfulness, both. Because Blissful Stickiness is more than being happy while messy. It's a state of mind. From now on, we want all the tactile sensations and heavenly moods to suffuse our basket-toting parties. From now on, we want to picnic like a heroine.

THE HISTORY OF THE PIQUE NIQUE

Centuries before Katy's molasses pies and Maya's secret sauce, there was a way of dining out of doors, but it wasn't called a "picnic."

Before the French glommed onto this concept of eating outside and making it fancy, the working classes were way ahead of them. In 1394, the epic poem "Pierce the Ploughman's Creed" mentions the traditional plowman's meal of bread, cheese, and beer. English rural laborers ate bread and cheese for centuries: skimmed-milk cheese, complemented with a schmear of lard and butter, was their main source of fats and protein. In lieu of mustard and mayo, onions were the condiment of choice. Luckily, those onions also gave the workers a pop of Vitamin C. At some point, pickles were incorporated into the plowman's lunch, adding a bang of dynamism and probiotics.

Honestly, fresh-baked bread, farm-churned butter, and homemade cheese sounds like a small feast to us, the solid makings of a simple-yet-scrummy picnic. But of course, we modern picnic goers don't have to arise from our lunch and drag a plow through a muddy, blazing-hot field of turnips for sweaty hours on end. The original (pre-word) picnics were not exactly picnics. So how ever did we come to the charming tableau we clasp to our collective bosoms, of wicker baskets, red-checked tablecloths, baguettes, and wedges of blue-veined cheese?

Merci to the French, for it was they who designed picnicking as we know it. The English word "picnic" comes from the French term "pique-nique," which was used from the mid-1600s on to describe epicures who brought their own wine when dining out. This evolved into a potluck of sorts, in which people would bring their own wine and their own food, but it would still be an indoor thing for a long time.

Where "picnic" comes from is something of a mystery. Drilled down from the original French "pique-nique," the word was likely invented by joining the common form of the verb "piquer" (meaning "to pick" or "peck") with "nique," possibly either a Germanic term meaning "trifle," or merely a nonsense rhyming syllable to twin with the first part of the word.

Could "to pick" mean "be selective" about "trifles," or maybe frivolous foods that one wouldn't eat every day? Or do we just crave a scoop of beauteous English trifle with berries and custard?

In a bit of a plot twist, the picnic moved out into the open air. After the French Revolution, many of our friends the Pique-nique-ers ran for their lives, most of them to England, where, strapped for cash, they did their best to maintain the foodways of their homeland on the cheap. One way was to lay out a blanket and tote a basket of fruit, bread, cheese, cold meats, and wine to a picturesque spot.

We think we know what happened next: the Brits noticed and wanted in on this chic way of enjoying a meal, *au grand air*. By 1808, picnicking had taken on a genteel air, and the upper crust were writing about it in their books and journals.

By the time our heroine Jane Austen was detailing Emma's picnic at Box Hill in 1816, picnicking was posh doings that required hours of laborious effort behind the scenes:

"These elegant and sumptuous picnics were not easy to accomplish," according to the Jane Austen's World blog. "Teams of horses were arranged to transport wagons with picnickers, servants, food, and outdoor furniture. If the picturesque spot was located in an out of the way place, the party had to walk the remainder of the way with the supplies. The servants would lay out the dishes, and tables and cloths al fresco. After the parties had dined, these supplies needed to be repacked."

Yeah, nobody was having a good time at Emma's Box Hill picnic—not the servants, lugging 1806 bento boxes full of cold pigeon pie, not Emma, and certainly not that poor lamb Miss Bates. Not even picnicking can save a scenario underlaid with unfortunate emotional undercurrents. Not even Maya's secret sauce and Katy's molasses pies could have rescued Emma from herself. Mood: the opposite of Blissful Stickiness—miserable and troubled! As Emma shows us, you may emerge from a picnic un-sticky, with clean hands, but if you have a cold heart, it's all been for naught.

HEROINE TAKEAWAYS

● BEGIN YOUR NEXT PICNIC WITH A TOAST: In the final pages of *Little Women*, we find the March family in the apple orchard at Plumfield "on a mellow October day, when the air was full of an exhilarating freshness which made the spirits rise, and the blood dance health-ily in the veins". Ah, a fall picnic! Professor Bhaer, professing his gratitude, raises a glass to the memory of cranky but generous Aunt March. And thus begins a hearty round of brief toasts, to the elation of all. In the moment, a toast may seem like more trouble than it's worth. Especially if you are an introvert, intentionally inviting all attention to yourself so that your words may be heard is an easy thing to "pass" on. But proposing a toast is actually much easier than, say, arranging the proper decor or providing live music. That is, it's the simplest way to set the mood! Formal or informal, a brief toast of thankfulness at the beginning of a gathering is the perfect way to quickly and effectively establish a welcoming setting among friends, family, or strangers.

● DON'T FRET ABOUT YOUR COOKING SKILLS: It's a fact that every-thing tastes better outside. When Clara's Grandmama joins Clara and Heidi for a meal in the Alps, she is shocked (and pleased) to see Clara, who in previous chapters merely picked at her food, reach for a second helping of cheese. Clara exclaims that it tastes better than anything they ate back home, and Grandfather declares good naturedly, "Don't stop, our mountain wind helps along where the cooking is faulty!" Would it be too much to advise that the next time you burn dinner, move your dinner party outside and proclaim it edible? All we're saying is, it can't hurt.

● BRING SOMETHING NEW TO TRY: For Anne Shirley, the excitement of her first picnic tipped into "sublime" territory at the mere idea of trying ice cream for the first time. Ice cream and picnics go together like Gilbert Blythe and a cracked slate (an iconic pairing), but a picnic is also the perfect opportunity to try a new food, or a food you may be familiar with in its more natural state (like a honeycomb), a jar of something you've picked up at a local ethnic market (like kimchi), or a sampling of imported candy (like Kinder Chocolate).

○ SEEK AND FIND BEAUTY LIKE ANNE AND CO.: In *Anne of Avonlea*, Anne, Diana, Priscilla, and Jane set out to the remotest pockets of the woods to enjoy a golden spring picnic in celebration of Anne's birthday. Anne, as Diana poignantly points out, was not actually born in spring, but Anne retorts that she would have been born in spring if she had had any say in the matter.

"It must be delightful to come into the world with the mayflowers and violets. You would always feel that you were their foster sister."

Diana, satisfied with this reasoning, agrees to come to Green Gables early Saturday morning to help prepare a lunch of "the daintiest things possible...things that will match the spring, you understand." The picnic basket is thus fitted with jelly tarts, drop cookies—frosted with pink and yellow icing—buttercup cake, lemonade, and...sandwiches. (Anne admits the prosaic necessity of sandwiches here, naming them for what they are: "unpoetical.")

On the day of the picnic, as the merry party is parading to the perfect picnic location, Anne, in the most Anne-ish way, makes a wonderful suggestion: "Let's try to make this a really golden day, girls, a day to which we can always look back with delight. We're to seek for beauty and refuse to see anything else."

Shortly after, when Anne spots a delightful cluster of violets, she vows to keep the image in her memory bank for the rest of her time on this earth.

"'I'm so glad we came this way,' said Anne, the shining-eyed. 'This is my adopted birthday, you know, and this garden and its story is the birthday gift it has given me.'"

What is stopping any of us from adopting a beautiful day in our favorite season to be our "rightful birthday," going about expecting to receive a great gift, and then gratefully accepting it when it presents itself? A picnic would be the perfect setting for such a state of mind. Or is it a picnic state of mind that sets the stage for a perfect day of receiving beautiful gifts?

- DON'T GO OVERBOARD LIKE THE VICTORIANS: We already knew that the Victorians were bananas for picnics, but we didn't know how bananas until we read the basket-packing list for the ideal period picnic from *Mrs. Beeton's Book of Household Management*. Mrs. Beeton was the Ina Garten or Betty Crocker of her day, and heroines such as author Frances Hodgson Burnett (*A Secret Garden*) and Meg March (*Little Women*) would have been heavily influenced by her cookbook. Keep in mind her suggested menu is for forty people, but still, we have to wonder if Mrs. Beeton was quite well in the head. Her picnic menu includes many meat joints, meat pies, lobsters, breads, cakes, biscuits, and half a tin of tea. It includes "1 epic of collared calf's head," which Lorilee unfortunately Googled. Mrs. Beeton, what were you drinking, lady? She also advises not to tote along any coffee, being "not suitable for a picnic, being difficult to make." Brewing tea on a grassy knoll was easy, but apparently coffee was beyond the pale. Our point: Keep your picnic party manageable and avoid disembodied animal heads whenever possible.

- PICK A SETTING LIKE A HEROINE: The heroines truly did have some enchanting locations for their open-air meals, a la Katy's "Paradise." Esperanza of *Esperanza Rising* "spread a blanket on the ground, then unwrapped a bundle of burritos, avocados and grapes...in view of golden hills." Other literary picnic locales include meadows, orchards, mountainsides, verdant parklands, and babbling brooks perfect for chilling one's ginger beer.

In *Little Women*, Laurie invites the March sisters to join him and his English guests to a lavish luncheon on the meadow, complete with separate tents for cooking and dining. The novel ends with a much simpler, rustic picnic in the apple orchard, with blankets on the ground, sandwiches, apple turnovers, and pickles.

In *The Secret Garden Cookbook*, author Amy Cotler gives insight into the settings of our heroine's picnics. "For the wealthy, they often include journeys into attractive landscapes," she writes. "At a fashionable picnic, the ladies might sketch the scenery while the gentlemen looked for archeological remains or wild mushrooms." Emma's Box Hill would have been one such attractive landscape, featuring box trees, flowers, bird song, and fully two-thirds of the British butterfly species (true story).

Let's say for argument's sake that your picnic site is sadly lacking in fully two-thirds of the British butterfly species. You can still find a lush, green spot in the shade, knowing that even a slight change of scenery—out of doors—is all it takes to expand one's heart and soul.

◉ MAKE IT MARVELOUS: In their lustrous book *The Picnic*, the ladies of the Portland Picnic Society offer a bounty of ideas for elevating your meal-on-a-blanket to something radiant. All it takes is a special treat or surprise here and there to add some lumens (units of light) to your fresh air feast. Tote your ordinary foodstuffs in tiffins (Indian high-rise, stackable lunch pails), or pack a cake plate to pile your sandwiches with panache. Bring a wooden cutting board and some fancy charcuterie (three slices of each meat per person) and some swanky little cheeses you wouldn't normally partake of. At Lorilee's last picnic, she sprung for a luscious artichoke dip that more than absolved the rather humdrum crackers of their ordinariness. String twinkly lights in the trees. Make dessert your most luminous course, with homemade peach cobbler or store-bought pavlovas. Or bring a bag of vintage candy from your favorite sweet shop. After all, as the authors note, "nobody is going to kick you off the blanket for bringing chocolate." Finally, grab a bottle of something bubbly and festive, and drink it there on your blanket, happy and lit up with picnic lumens from the inside out.

● DON'T FORGET TO BRING CHILDREN: According to Louisa May Alcott in *Little Women*, an altogether "excellent person [with whom] to carry on a picnic" is someone "not very wise, but very good-natured." This is likely because a picnic is far from practical. Dining at a table not far from the kitchen, without the distraction of the outdoors, is a far more efficient way of staving off hunger, to be sure. But if it's true that the best Picnicking Partner is a little foolish and very amiable, who better to invite on your next outdoor eating adventure than a child? Parents, aunts, grandmothers: just think! Not only do children delight in eating anywhere outside the bounds of a kitchen, but when eating outside, crumbs become irrelevant, "weird" foods become intriguing, the plight of the short order cook is obliterated, and "getting up from the table" is actually encouraged. It's a mercy for both children and adults, and a chance for children to see their grownups in a fresh light. (Bonus points for organizing a search for dryads in the trees, post dessert.)

● PICNIC FOR PERSONAL GROWTH: What do the picnic scenes of *What Katy Did, Emma,* and *Anne of Green Gables* all have in common? Literarily speaking, they all signify pivotal moments for a character or characters, foreshadowing the beginning of a shift in perspective.

In *Emma,* we see Emma in a new light as she reveals her worst moment in the book on Box Hill, signaling to the reader that not only is a change needed, but a change is coming. How hopeful!

For Katy and co., their picnic comes after a long winter, and helps the reader settle into a childlike point of view: suddenly we, too, see the swampy thicket in early spring as akin to fairyland, as well as the perfect spot to each lunch. But the picnic setting is also the paradise from which

Katy eventually *falls* (forgive us, but it's not often metaphor and spoiler come together so seamlessly). It is here where she promises to "head a crusade and ride on a white horse, with armor and a helmet on my head, and carry a sacred flag," or in some similar fashion, be an "ornament to the family." She does make her family proud, but not without a difficult lesson in humility first.

For Anne, the Sunday school picnic is not just wish-fulfillment for a community-starved orphan, but a crucial moment in the way Marilla views her red-headed Christian-duty-personified. Marilla forbade Anne to attend the picnic because she believed Anne had stolen her most prized possession, a false accusation Anne wasn't sure she would survive. Marilla soon realizes she was wrong, however, and the two are reconciled and the punishment is reneged. As she traipses off with a basket of baked goods over her arm, Anne is soaring on the wings of being truly seen, and Marilla has an inkling of something she will come to understand much more as the novel progresses: that maybe she needs Anne as much as Anne needs her.

So consider this an invitation to view The Picnic as a literary tool in the plot development of your own life. What a lovely lesson from the heroines: that good company, a few delicious trifles, and a dash of out-of-the-ordinary, is often all we need to remember that there is more to the story than our limited point of view. Isn't it splendid to think of picnicking as the practice of seeing the world like a heroine: full of blissfully sticky possibilities?

HEROINE CHALLENGE

Start Where You Are

If you've never planned a picnic before, remember again the words of Maya: do the best you can until you know better. Flex your visions of lounging under blooming bowers and nibbling on carefully prepared puffed pastry desserts. "Blissful stickiness" is the goal, so aim to create the kind of picnic that feels truly "you" in the end (and it may take practice—but that's part of the fun). Your picnic plans shouldn't cause a headache but planning it will require effort. Whether your dream picnic requires a proper wicker basket and real china, or a smattering of store-bought foods you've never tried before on paper plates, challenge yourself to gather what you need with fresh eyes. Dust off your "saving this for a special occasion" serving dish, or search thrift stores for unique finds to further set apart your outdoor eating experience. Some things to look for: old quilts and brightly colored blankets, tiffins, mason and parfait jars, thermoses, wooden cutting boards, and Radio Flyer wagons to move your feast to an inspiring location.

JENNY'S FETA PASTA SALAD

(from Author Ina Garten)

At first glance this pasta salad appears complicated, but it comes together easily, and the reward is great for a small investment. A bounty of colorful vegetables, perfect in their roasted sweetness, blend beautifully with the saltiness of the feta cheese and the acidity of the lemon. Bring this along to your picnic with a few simple sides and your meal will feel elevated and complete.

YIELD: 6-8 SERVINGS

INGREDIENTS

1 small eggplant, peeled, and diced into ¾ inch cubes
1 red bell pepper, 1-inch diced
1 yellow pepper, 1-inch diced
1 red onion peeled, 1-inch diced
2 garlic cloves, minced
⅓ C olive oil
1 ½ tsp. salt
½ tsp. freshly ground black pepper
½ lb. orzo pasta

FOR THE DRESSING

⅓ C freshly squeezed lemon juice (about two lemons)
⅓ C olive oil
1 tsp. salt
½ tsp. freshly ground black pepper

(continues on next page)

4 scallions minced (white and green parts)
¼ C toasted pignolis (pine nuts)
¾ C feta, diced
15 fresh basil leaves, cut into julienne (thin strips)

INSTRUCTIONS

1. Preheat oven to 425 degrees F (218 C).

2. Toss the eggplant, bell peppers, onion, and garlic with the olive oil, salt, and pepper on a large sheet pan. Roast for 40 minutes, until browned, turning once with a spatula.

3. Meanwhile, cook the orzo in boiling salted water for 7 to 9 minutes, until tender. Drain and transfer to a large serving bowl. Add the roasted vegetables to the pasta, scraping all the liquid and seasonings from the roasting pan into the pasta bowl.

4. For the dressing, combine the lemon juice, olive oil, salt, and pepper and pour on the pasta and vegetables. Let cool to room temperature, then add the scallions, pignolis, feta, and basil. Check the seasonings and serve at room temperature.

What are your favorite picnic foods?

....

....

....

....

....

....

....

....

....

....

....

....

....

....

....

....

....

⋮ HEROINE comfort ⋮
F O O D S

POLLYANNA'S
CALF'S-FOOT JELLY

MRS. JENNINGS'S
"every delicacy
in the house"

MAYA'S
MOMMA'S
CARAMEL
CAKE

MEG MARCH'S BLANCMANGE

ESPERANZA'S ROSE
HIP TEA

MILK

BUTTER

LOGAN FAMILY'S
MEAL TO THE BERRYS

Chapter 2

COMFORT LIKE A HEROINE

Bring Mostly Soup, with the Occasional Bowl of Pollyanna's Calf's Foot Jelly

"Where we're going, the man is very sick and he doesn't look like other people. But I don't want you to be afraid or uncomfortable when you see him. Just be yourselves."

MARY LOGAN, "MAMA," *ROLL OF THUNDER, HEAR MY CRY.*

PROBLEM: How do we help bear the burdens of our loved ones in times of sickness and pain? How can we show up stronger for them and become more compassionate, comforting, and supportive? You want to do more for your people during challenging times, whether they are brokenhearted or convalescing, welcoming a new baby or moving to a new neighborhood. You want to go beyond check-in texts and the occasional phone call but need inspiration more timeless than Pinterest.

HEROINE SOLUTION: The heroines are full of age-old wisdom long forgotten and well-worth revisiting, from the healing benefits of collagen broth to long walks in the open air as a tonic for broken heartedness. You will learn how to deepen your bonds with your friends and loved ones, become more thoughtful, compassionate, and supportive as you learn to comfort like a heroine.

OUR HEROINES KNEW the healing power of food and drink, not just to mend the body but to soothe a broken heart, too.

Jane Austen's heroines administered "basins of soup." Cassie Logan of *Roll of Thunder, Hear My Cry* carried "cans of milk and butter, not to mention a jar of beef and a jar of crowder peas which Mama and Big Ma had canned" to an ailing victim of racial violence. And In *Sense and Sensibility*, when that caddish Willoughby rejected Marianne in favor of the wealthy Miss Grey, Mrs. Jennings sought to cure her broken heart with olives and dried cherries.

Showing compassion and care through food is as old as "invalid cookery" and as new as bringing a bowl of Pho or a smoothie to a sick, injured, grieving, or heartbroken friend or a dear one who could use a meal as a show of support and love.

Julia A. Pye, author of *Invalid Cookery: a Manual of Recipes for the Preparation of Food for the Sick and Convalescent; to Which is Added a Chapter of Practical Suggestions for the Sick-Room* (1880), addresses those attending to the "comfort and pleasure of suffering invalids."

Ms. Pye's thorough guide was written during an interesting time of transition in medical history. During the nineteenth century (when many of our heroines were written into existence), there was a gradual shift taking place as medical practices became professionalized. Whereas for most of the century, hospitals were primarily serving the poor and marginalized, and home care was reserved for the middle and upper classes, we see in the late 1800s fewer and fewer people being treated at home. Pye's first readers would have been quite familiar with the idea of home care, but perhaps beginning to think of serving their sick friends as better left to the professionals. Attending to the sick as a "sacred obligation" was far from a new idea, but perhaps at risk of fading from the collective imagination.

Fast forward nearly one and a half centuries, and Dr. Kelli Harding, in her book, *The Rabbit Effect: Live Longer, Happier, and Healthier with the Groundbreaking Science of Kindness* (2019), argues that we are missing some crucial pieces in our quest for overall health and well-being: "Factors like love, friendship, and dignity." Had she been able to, Ms. Pye would likely have written a glowing endorsement for Harding's book.

The heroines, along with kindred spirits Ms. Pye and Dr. Harding, invite us to consider the unique role that we, as friends and family, play in the health of our bedridden and grieving friends. While we may not be able to offer a diagnosis or prescribe medication, when we think like a heroine, there are countless ways in which we can contribute to the health of our loved ones. For where we bring comfort, pleasure, and kindness, we bring so much more: we reinforce the dignity of our friends in pain, and thereby fulfill our "sacred obligation."

When it comes to considering the mental, emotional, and physical well-being of a recovering friend, we can think of no better example than the heroine we mostly associate with lifting people's spirits, but whose name, we would argue strongly, might be more synonymous with "gelatin obsessed," than "overly positive." (In her defense, we think that latter attribution a woeful oversimplification.)

We are thinking of Pollyanna, of course, who never entered a sickroom without bearing a quivering, gelatinous bowl of calf's foot jelly (we have found multiple references to this appalling jelly; the heroines are quite obsessed).

Pollyanna had a last name—Whittier—but because her first name has become so synonymous with positivity, it's enough to say

"Pollyanna," and everyone knows who she is. Like so many of our heroines, Pollyanna was an orphan sent to live with challenging—at least at first—folk. In this case, Pollyanna dwelled with her crabby-pants Aunt Polly, who would never shirk her duty, even though she really wanted to. But Aunt Polly was no match for Pollyanna. In time, Pollyanna's glowing good vibes take the whole town of Beldingsville, Vermont, by storm, until everyone is seeing the bright side of things, including the crotchety Mrs. Snow, who eventually develops quite a hankering for Pollyanna's ministrations *vis-à-vis* calf's foot jelly.

Calf's-foot jelly? It is an old-fashioned jelly made from gelatin obtained by boiling calves' feet. One source we found suggested that it be served cold as an appetizer or "as a cool snack."

You know, just nibbling on a cool little slab of meat jelly over here.

"Garnish with a slice of lemon wedge," the instructions add, in case you are the type of person who garnishes their snacks.

We are not sure if Pollyanna boiled the calves' feet herself or not (likely a servant did this), but every time she toted a trembling bowl of hot collagen to Mrs. Snow, she brought more than soup. Comfort, compassion, and reassurance were in every spoonful.

In one scene, Pollyanna goes to visit Mrs. Snow in a "darkened room," and in her basket are nestled three kinds of healing foods: lamb broth, chicken broth, and calf's foot jelly. By her third visit, Mrs. Snow had a clear favorite—the jelly—and hailed Pollyanna's bowlful with gladness, not knowing that "the minister's wife had already that day sent over a great bowlful of that same kind of jelly." Obviously, the whole town was possessed by meat jellies.

Thankfully, this jelly-lovin' lady recovered, in no small part to Pollyanna's service. It just goes to show, a little care—even for someone who may not exactly deserve it—goes a long way.

WHY COLLAGEN IS THE GIFT THAT KEEPS ON GIVING

It's not hard to understand why the heroines perceived foods-that-jiggle as both elixirs and foolproof tokens of friendship, considering that peoples of every nation and every culture throughout history have used the healing powers of bone broth to prevent illness and nurture the sick. While the ubiquity of Campbell's soup in the early 1900s contributed to the decline of the making of homemade broth in the American kitchen, around the world it remains a practical and economical way to make use of cooked animal bones and vegetable scraps. And while the commendations for bone broth are nearly endless, its greatest virtue, as Pollyanna was well aware, is the collagen it contains.

In their book *Nourishing Broth*, Sally Fallon Morell and Kaayla T. Daniel, PhD, CCN write, "Collagen is the glue that holds the body together. The word comes from *kolla*, the Greek word for glue..." Animal bones, ligaments, and connective tissue are rich in collagen, and the best way to extract this priceless protein is to boil these animal parts in water.

It's as though the heroines simply knew in their *bones* that gelatinous broths and custards were the perfect tonics for everything from crankiness to sore throats, but modern science proves their (very healthy) guts were correct in their intuitions. The authors of *Nourishing Broth* go on to say that "the abundance of collagen in all types of bone broth" not only supports the heart, vision, digestion, gut health, and bolstering our immune system, it "even contributes to emotional stability and a positive mental attitude." So *that* is why Pollyanna was so insistent on delivering her collagen-rich gift to cantankerous Mrs. Snow!

As Fallon Morell and Daniel so eloquently put it, "there's a synergy in broth that simmers with a healing power far greater than the sum of its parts."

BLANCMANGE, ANYONE?

Another healing heroine story involving collagen is that of *Little Women*'s Jo March, who brought over a covered dish of her sister Meg's blancmange for her neighbor Laurie when he was feeling sick.

"Blancmange," write the authors of *The Little Women Cookbook*, "is a delicate milk pudding which was served as both a dessert and a food for the sick. It has faded almost entirely from the standard American diet, but it was enormously popular in Victorian times." (Martha Stewart calls it a large form panna cotta, and we defer to her!)

Jo brought Laurie some bland, sweet food, and her sister Beth's three kittens because Beth "thought her cats would be comforting," and they were. The book tells us that Laurie got over his shyness and "grew sociable."

He had already gleaned solace from the visit, and he hadn't even tried the blancmange, decorated with greenery and red flower petals from little sister Amy's geranium. When Laurie protested that the dish looks too good to eat, Jo demurred: "It isn't anything, only they all felt kindly, and wanted to show it. Tell the girl to put it away for your tea: it's so simple you can eat it; and being soft, it will slip down without hurting your sore throat."

INVALID CARE AT ITS FINEST

When this book was but a twinkle in our eyes, I (Lorilee) had the chance to bring a small package of TLC to my friend Tacy, named for Tacy of the beloved *Betsy Tacy* series by Maud Hart Lovelace. Darling Tacy—kind, loving, and cheerful to her friends—had somehow broken her ankle in a bad fall in her garage. My care package was simple: A cheery yellow mug—never used and purloined at a thrift shop, from my overstocked mug collection—a batch of ginger Tea Drops (dissolvable tea cakes in fun shapes), and a cute little stir stick in the shape of a beehive. Soon we were deep in conversation, settled in her squashy couch with mugs of steaming tea. Hopefully my friend was able to forget about her pain for a little while, but at the very least, her day was made brighter. To be honest, *my* day was made brighter as I reflected on how good it felt to care for a friend who had always cared for me.

On another occasion, I was the one being comforted with food. During Christmas of 2021, my husband, son, and I all came down with Covid. My husband had it the worst of us—his fever spiked to 104 degrees, and he was a moaning mass of misery on the couch.

Luckily, I had a less-severe case, even though I felt like I had been hit by a truck. Enter my husband's sister, Jodi, who drove almost an hour to our house bearing gorgeous chicken noodle soup—steamy, brothy, collagen-rich, and scrumptious—some beautiful fresh oranges, and other assorted grocery items such as bread and lunch meat. It was a godsend all the way around. We could barely stay awake, never mind cook for ourselves or anyone else. We ate off that big rubber container tub of soup for days, and then it was so nice to have a few groceries on hand to supplement the soup. That soup was crafted with care; I could feel it in my aching bones. It was invalid care at its finest. Beyond the practical issues of us three housebound sickies having something to eat, our souls gratefully received the healing and compassionate wishes cooked in.

A couple of months later, I found out that Doyle's cousin's daughter, who lived about fifteen minutes from us but an hour from her parents, had gotten Covid. Remembering how comforting Jodi's care package had been, I decided to pay it forward. I don't have Jodi's kitchen skills (she is literally a lunch lady!), nor did I have time to make a homemade soup. So I did what I could do at the time, which was pick up a jar of quality chicken noodle soup and a few nice oranges. Perusing my mug collection, I felt it was destiny when I spotted a mug with the letter M for our cousin's last name. I topped off the small parcel of solicitude with a few new bags of sore throat tea from the tea canister and hopped in my car to deliver the goods to Cousin Miller's front door. Soon afterward,

I got a text with lots of smiley faces and exclamation points, and the promise that the currently stricken young lady would pay it forward too when she recovered.

 ## FOOD FOR THE HEARTSICK

Cherries wearing nightgowns. Healing Caramel Cake. Southern crowder peas. This quirky trio of edibles all have one thing in common: our favorite literary ladies employed them in their attempts to comfort like a heroine.

Because sometimes a heroine is called upon to bring empathy, gladdening, help, and relief to someone who has a fractured heart.

Take Mrs. Jennings, the hearty lady in *Sense and Sensibility*, who, following the cold jilting of Marianne by that gold-digger Willoughby, prescribed not fluids and meat jellies, but dainty gourmet tidbits.

Poor Marianne! Although, we don't feel too sorry for her because we know this too shall pass and soon, she will be all "Willoughby who?" and "Hey there, Colonel Brandon." Still, the dear lamb is suffering, that much is clear. As she sits there "looking most wretchedly," in a stupor of foggy heartache, she is oblivious to the fact that Mrs. Jennings noted her unhappiness and "felt that every thing was due to her which might make her at all less so." Marianne is parked by the fire, and plied with "every delicacy in the house," including sweetmeats, olives, Constantia wine, and dried cherries. But alas, Marianne's misery was too intense to be mitigated by *cherries en chemise*, a specialty recipe of the day involving dried cherries enrobed in meringue like tiny, fluffy white nightgowns.

"'Poor soul!' cried Mrs. Jennings, as soon as she was gone, 'how it grieves me to see her! And I declare if she is not gone away without finishing her wine! And the dried cherries too! Lord! nothing seems to do her any good. I am sure if I knew of any thing she would like, I would send all over the town for it.'"

We feel that Mrs. Jennings's warm heart was in the right place, even though she was a little bit *much* in her efforts. That good lady jumped in with both feet to bring a spot of cheer to a grim scenario. The message at the core of Mrs. Jennings's efforts was this: "I care about you. And I am going to show up for you and try and make you feel special—even though that scoundrel W made you feel the opposite." We guess that it did work on some level, and we're not alone.

"It used to seem ridiculous to me for her to think that delicious, sweet Muscat wine from Constantia, dried cherries or olives could help mend Marianne's broken heart," writes Pen Vogler, the author of several Jane Austen-related cookbooks. "I now think it is ridiculous of Marianne not to think that they would at least help."

The Comfort of Caramel Cake

Maya Angelou was not only a radiant writer, but also a famously good cook. No doubt her love for culinary pursuits was passed down by her beloved grandmother, "Momma," who "knew just what to do for everything," says Angelou. "And it would always have to do with food."

In one of her cookbooks, *Hallelujah!*, Angelou writes about a time in her life when her Momma helped heal her from a humiliating situation through a luscious and labor-intensive caramel cake.

The essay "The Assurance of Caramel Cake" shows how food can restore the soul as well as the body. A traditional American layer cake with Southern roots, Momma's Caramel Cake was always to be spoken of in capital letters, and took four or five hours to make, a period which included Momma calibrating the fire at a particular heat on her wood stove. "The salty sweetness of the caramel frosting along with the richness of the batter made the dessert soften and liquefy on the tongue and slip quietly down the throat almost without notice," she wrote. "Save that it left a memory of heaven itself in the mouth."

⬤ BE YOURSELF: Cassie Logan is the ten-year-old first person narrator of *Roll of Thunder, Hear My Cry*, the 1977 Newberry Prize winner by Mildred Taylor. Set in Mississippi at the height of the Depression, this is the story of one family's struggle to maintain their honor, dignity, and flourishing in the face of racism and social injustice. No discussion of comforting like a heroine would be complete without the story of how Cassie, her mama, and siblings brought nourishing food to a victim of racially motivated violence. The Logan children were woken before dawn, and their mama prepared them for what is to come. "Where we're going, the man is very sick and he doesn't look like other people. But I don't want you to be afraid or uncomfortable when you see him. Just be yourselves."

This would prove to be a tall order, as "ancient" Mr. Berry had been burned alive and was a grotesque version of his former self. Mrs. Berry was thrilled by the visit. "Land sakes, child, ain't you somethin'!?" she exclaimed. "Comin' to see bout' these old bones. I just sez' to Sam, I sez, 'Who you reckon comin to see old folks like us?'"

Cassie's mama was really the heroine in this story. She modeled for her children how to care for neighbors in terrible distress. Cassie, who stands her ground in many scary and threatening situations, has another opportunity to be brave when she witnesses Mr. Berry's horrific reality. The nourishing food brought—canned milk, butter and beef, and a jar of crowder peas—would nurture the bodies of Mr. and Mrs. Berry, but it was the Logan family's courage and care that infused the offerings with so much more. It showed this poor man and his wife that someone cared—they were not alone.

Cassie's mama also gave her children—and us—golden advice for any situation that might make us uncomfortable. "Just be yourself." It can be hard to be in situations where someone is suffering terribly. Showing up is half the battle, and it's hard to know how to act around the sick and dying. But as we learn from this story, presence and authenticity can feel just as comforting as a bowl of chicken noodle soup—or a jar of crowder peas.

- CREATE A COMFORTING PANTRY: We consider soup to pretty much be the sixth love language. We also believe the first step to a well-prepared pantry (of freezer, or fridge) is believing you have something unique to offer when it comes to making your friends feel loved. So press pause and, before you turn elsewhere for inspiration, take a moment to consider your own special gifts.

Maybe you regularly bake cookies with your kids. You might consider freezing a few dough balls from every batch, in order to have a variety of options at the ready when time is limited in the future. Or maybe you loathe baking but are unintimidated by whipping up a batch of chicken liver pâté, which is practically alive with immune-boosting vitamins and minerals. (Don't let our use of "alive" scare you here if you've never tried pâté.)

Like Emily Dickinson, determine to dwell in possibility! "Being prepared" might look more like a variety of store-bought jams and an abundant supply of pretty stationery, on which you can use your poetic gifts to lift the spirits of someone you care about.

- CONNECT TO A LOST LOVED ONE: If one of your people has lost someone dear to them, consider bringing them a food or a drink that connects meaningfully with their loved one. This might mean bringing your friend's dad's favorite dessert or an ethnic food from the loved one's heritage.

We adore this example of comfort and connection from the modern classic *Esperanza Rising* by Pam Muñoz Ryan, a book written in 2000 but set in the 1930s in Mexico, just after the Mexican revolution. Our heroine, Esperanza, whose father has been murdered, excuses herself from the company of others to go sit on a stone bench in Papa's garden.

"Many of the roses had dropped their petals, leaving the stem and the rosehip, the green grape like fruit of the rose. Abuelita said the rosehip contained the memory of the roses, and when you drank tea made from it, you took in all the beauty the plant had known. These roses had known Papa, she thought. She would ask Hortensia to make rosehip tea tomorrow." Esperanza drew comfort from the steamy warmth and aroma of the rosehip tea, an experience that would always keep the memory of her father close to her.

HEROINE CHALLENGE
BE PREPARED

Be prepared to show compassion at any time. Scope out thrift stores and garage sales for charming mugs, spoons, ladles, and bedside bells. Buy a few "get well soon" or condolence cards so you will have them on hand to go with your foodie care. Next time you make a sustaining soup, make enough to freeze a second batch. Stock your heroine's pantry with soup stock, canned beans, and other soup fixings. Be prepared in other, less tangible ways by paying attention to what might best comfort a friend or loved one. Ask questions that are easy to answer, such as "What is your favorite comfort food?" "What food do you associate with your loved one?" and "Are there any food sensitivities or allergies I should know about?" Don't put it on the sick, convalescing, or grieving person to tell you what to do, ala "Let me know if there is anything you need." Experts say that just adds to their burden.

Recipe

CASSIE LOGAN'S CROWDER PEAS

A Southern soul food staple, crowder peas are easy to cook and great with fresh tomatoes!

INGREDIENTS

2 C crowder peas

4 C chicken broth

Fat of choice: 1 Tbsp. bacon grease *or* 1 oz. salt pork *or* 1 Tbsp. jarred ham base

¼ tsp. dried thyme

Kosher salt and black pepper, to taste

INSTRUCTIONS

1. Put the crowder peas in a pot and cover with chicken broth.

2. Add in your fat and the dried thyme.

3. Bring the mixture to a boil over medium-high heat then reduce heat to low and simmer for 15 to 20 minutes, until peas are tender but not overcooked.

4. Drain and place in a bowl. Taste and add salt and black pepper as needed.

5. Once the beans have cooled slightly, add in the chopped tomatoes and green onions, then taste and add salt and pepper if needed. Serve with hot sauce.

"To be ALLOWED, no, invited, INTO THE PRIVATE LIVES of strangers, AND to share THEIR joys AND FEARS, was a CHANCE... for a cup of mead WITH BEOWULF OR A HOT cup of tea and milk WITH Oliver Twist."

—MAYA ANGELOU

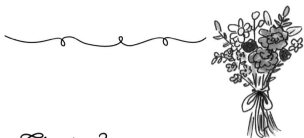

Chapter 3

OFFER PINAFORE HOSPITALITY LIKE A HEROINE

LEARN THE ART OF EVERYDAY HOSPITALITY AND YOUR GUESTS WILL FEEL WELCOME AND INVITED

"The etymology of the word *companion* means a person who breaks bread with another…It points to the power of bread to build relationships in unexpected ways."

KENDALL VANDERSLICE, *BY BREAD ALONE*

PROBLEM: Most of us don't often have people over. We may just feel uncomfortable with the idea, but more than likely, hosting feels like an "extra" that can only happen once we have our lives together. We feel lonely

and disconnected, however, and lament the fact that it seems so difficult to bring together our neighbors, school moms, church and work
friends, and book club pals to connect on a more meaningful level. We
admire old-fashioned hospitality practices, such as welcoming a friend
who has dropped in unannounced, and wonder how to make space for
casual, everyday hospitality in our hyper-individualistic and busy lives.

HEROINE SOLUTION: The heroines teach us how to be ready and openhearted for everyday hospitality opportunities, and to confidently open
our homes to guests long before conditions are perfect. You will learn
to start where you are and learn the "craft of love," developing an invitational attitude. You will be armed with practical tips for spontaneous
and casual hosting which will increase your own sense of belonging and
connection to others.

SUNDAY NIGHT LUNCH at the Ray house? It's a yes from us, if only
to try out Mr. Ray's Swedish Egg Coffee and lounge around a roaring fire, belonging there with friends old and new.

We are talking about the beloved tradition enshrined in the *Betsy-Tacy* series by Minnesota writer Maud Hart Lovelace. (Is that not the
most perfect name for a person who wrote turn-of-the-century coming
of age novels?)

Betsy Ray was based on Maud's own life growing up in Mankato,
Minnesota. In this beguiling, ten-book series, Betsy is revealed to be
sociable, fun-loving, and highly imaginative. The first book, *Betsy-Tacy*,
begins in 1897 on the eve of Betsy's fifth birthday, and the last book,
Betsy's Wedding, ends in 1917 as the United States prepares to enter the
First World War. Do read the books if you haven't (or reread them if you
have), but for now, let's get back to Sunday evenings, when the Ray's
home became a haven of casual, "pinafore" hospitality.

A pinafore is a full apron with two holes for the arms that is tied or buttoned in the back, usually just below the neck. Alice in Wonderland and Pippi Longstocking famously wore them, and Jane Eyre was forced to make her own at Lowood School. Back in the day, it connoted kitchen work, but today's equivalent, since we don't usually wear aprons (unless you, like Jenny, are also trying to curb a vintage apron-buying habit), might be loungewear or Lorilee's Winnipeg Jets leggings. Something to wear if a neighbor dropped in for a visit or your kids's friends wanted to hang out at your house.

Even Bob Ray wore a pinafore (well, an apron) while presiding over Sunday Night Lunch. In *Heaven to Betsy,* the first mention of the ritual, we are told Sunday Night Lunch was nothing less than an "institution" at the Ray house.

"They never called it supper; and they scorned folks who called it tea. The drink of the evening was coffee, which Mrs. Ray loved, and although Betsy and Margaret still took cocoa, their loyalty was to coffee for her sake."

Mr. Ray, or Bob, if we are to be on a first name basis with him, preferred his coffee to be Swedish and made with eggs. Also known as "church basement coffee," Swedish egg coffee is made by adding a raw egg to the grounds before brewing, creating a potting soil-type texture. This process extracts bitterness from the grounds and brews a velvety, smooth cuppa Joe.

Velvety coffee sounds nice, but there was so much more to the Sunday Night Lunch.

In a role reversal rarely seen in a 1907 book, our heroine Bob—and yes, his actions elevate him to heroine—did all the cooking, if you can call it cooking. He whipped up all the food and drinks, or at least assembled it in the case of Anna's cakes (she was the hilarious cook/confidante). No one else was allowed to darken the door of the kitchen unless they wanted to watch and commend.

Bob was no dummy. He didn't "object" when Anna or his wife made a cake earlier in the day, and he didn't "mind" if his daughters draped a tablecloth over the dining room table. But he alone was king of the kitchen on Sunday nights.

As the coffee simmered, filling the kitchen with its aroma, Bob got to work on the sandwiches. Out came the breadboard, the knives, and the knife sharpener. After cutting the bread into slices, he rummaged in the icebox for whatever sandwich fixings he could find. Sometimes there was leftover roast beef or chicken from the big noon meal, or maybe cheese, or if all else failed, onions. Just onions! He sprinkled them with vinegar, and then powdered them judiciously with salt and pepper.

"I'm not," he said with sedate pride, "the sort of sandwich maker who puts salt and pepper all in one place with a shovel. No siree!" And then he would add, for emphasis, "No siree, BOB!"

(We just so badly want to jump into the fifth dimension and tesser on down to Minnesota, 1907, and give that aproned man a squeeze, how about you?)

The onion sandwiches were a huge hit with the boys who herded themselves to the Ray house for Sunday Night Lunch.

Here's where things got hospitable, because Bob Ray didn't mind a horde of teenage boys cramming into his space. In fact, he liked it. Also invited: he and Mrs. Ray's friends, and friends of Betsy and her sisters, and friends of their friends. Anyone could tag along, there was always room for one more guest. "Old and young gathered in the dining room around the table beneath the hanging lamp," doing justice, we assume, to the platter of sandwiches, the dish of pickles, and cake for dessert.

Which brings us to our favorite part of this whole paragon of heroine hospitality: "There was always a fire in the dining room grate for Sunday night lunch. Often the crowd spilled over to pillows ranged around the fire. Almost everyone ended there, with a second cup of coffee and his cake. Talk flourished, until Julia went to the piano. (And just to prove that his sense of humor was as flawless as his sandwich-making skills), Mr. Ray always made her play, 'Everybody Works but Father.'"

This gathering was based on Maud Hart Lovelace's own family tradition. Years later, when her "crowd" were grandpas and grandmas, they would tell her they still dreamed about her dad's onion sandwiches.

What they were likely dreaming about was the way they *felt* at the Ray house. Welcomed. Invited. Accepted. Like they belonged there, with the Rays and with each other. By inviting her readers to Sunday Night Lunch, Maud Hart Lovelace, Betsy, and Bob show us how to open our hearts and homes to friends and strangers alike. They teach us how to offer Pinafore Hospitality like a heroine.

READER, I INVITED HIM

We think it's high time the old-fashioned value of hospitality was resurrected, don't you? Living in our Western culture, developing an invitational mindset like the Rays is going against the grain, to say the least, but it can be done. In Western cultures, our default is privacy, individualism, and independence—not togetherness, curiosity about others, or leaning on the community for support.

It's no surprise to learn that the United States is listed as number one on the individualism index, a measure used by researchers to determine how where we live influences how we think about the role of the individual vs. the role of the group. In contrast, most countries in South and Central America, Africa, and Asia fall much lower on the list, valuing the group over the individual.

How does this rugged individualism play into our ideas of hospitality—or more to the point, lack of hospitality? When we are so tied to the idea that we can take care of ourselves, we don't want to even feel as if we need something from someone else. Then the subtle, yet insidious idea takes hold that others don't need us, either. People stick to themselves, clinging to the idea of self-sufficiency, and as a result, it's commonplace for neighbors to not know each other, even if they've lived across the street for ten years.

We are also obsessed with privacy, in a way that severely limits our opportunities to build community.

In her book *Invited,* writer Leslie Verner says real hospitality is not having a Pinterest-perfect table or well-appointed living room. True hospitality is not clean, comfortable, or controlled. It is an invitation to enter a sacred space together with friends and strangers.

"Privacy can be the enemy of the open home," she writes. "With such a high value on individualism and privacy, it's no wonder many of us in the West feel isolated and lonely."

Verner's words rang in my (Lorilee's) ears as I contemplated whether or not to allow my Chinese host daughter to invite her boyfriend, Moses, over after their half-day at school. It would be a seven-hour visit, and Elsa wanted to cook Chinese food for Moses's upcoming birthday. At first, I didn't want to say yes. It would be inconvenient, as I would have to supervise them at least a little bit. Our small kitchen would be subsumed for much of that time, and the house would smell like fish for hours afterward. Even if I asked Elsa to clean up everything afterwards, which I did, I knew there would be things for me to tidy up anyway. And when I wanted to come down for my coffee break, they would be there, in my space, giggling and watching movies on their phones.

Privacy can be the enemy of the open home. Well, darn it! I wanted to have an open home, but I also knew it would cost me a little bit. I also remembered the words of Pastor Peter Jonker, who came to one of our meetings of international host parents and spoke about hospitality. I had never thought of our hosting international students as an act of hospitality, but Peter cast a new vision for hosting that was expansive, a constant working out of the "craft of love." He told us that hospitality, which comes from the same word as "hospital," could be gritty and costly at times, words that have helped me many times over the last ten years as we have hosted now seventeen international students in our home.

Reader, I invited him. I know, it's not that big of a deal. But it *was* an inconvenience, *and* this small act of openheartedness strengthened my hospitality muscles. Hopefully, one floppy-haired Chinese teenager felt a little less lonely in our world, far from home. Now, I'm no Bob Ray, and I did not produce onion sandwiches, but I hope Moses felt at home here. Welcomed. Invited. Accepted. Like he belonged here, if only for seven hours on a simple Monday.

HEROINE TAKEAWAYS

- **EMBRACE THE ENCHANTMENT OF HOSPITALITY WITH MAYA ANGELOU:** In *I Know Why the Caged Bird Sings,* Maya Angelou writes about being invited over to Mrs. Flowers's house for tea, cookies, and lemonade—and a discussion about books.

Mrs. Flowers hadn't baked in a while, but she made some vanilla tea cookies for herself and young Maya to share for their book chat. Simple, but perfect. This invitation made a powerful impression on Maya, beginning with the scent of vanilla that greeted her at the door. The effect this interlude had on Maya never, ever went away.

"I have tried often to search behind the sophistication of years for the enchantment I so easily found in those gifts," she writes. "The essence escapes but its aura remains. To be allowed, no, invited, into the private lives of strangers, and to share their joys and fears, was a chance...for a cup of mead with Beowulf or a hot cup of tea and milk with Oliver Twist."

Sometimes, a few cookies, tea, and conversation are all it takes to "enchant" someone, making them feel understood, accepted, elevated, and honored.

- **MAKE THE BEST OF IT, LIKE KATY CARR:** An example of "gritty" hospitality arises in one of our favorite heroine novels, 1872's *What Katy Did* by Susan Coolidge. Since her mother has died, sixteen-year-old Katy must assume the mantle of household manager. One day, an unpleasant lady named Mrs. Worrett showed up at their door, unannounced. The Carr's maid, Bridget, gives Katy the option to send Mrs. Worrett away. But Katy makes the "considerate" choice:

"We must just make the best of it," Katy tells Bridget. Casual hospitality can require a certain amount of improvisation, and Katy improvises: "Run down, Clover, dear, that's a good girl! and tell Mrs. Worrett that the dining-room is all in confusion, but that we're going to have lunch here, and, after she's rested, I should be glad to have her come up. And, oh, Clovy! give her a fan the first thing. She'll be so hot. Bridget, you can bring up the luncheon just the same, only take out some canned peaches, by way of a dessert, and make Mrs. Worrett a cup of tea. She drinks tea always, I believe."

Mrs. Worrett stayed and stayed, for hours. It was boring, tedious, and awkward, but this heroine rose above it all. Katy and her siblings had no idea what to say to this tiresome lady with her nonstop prattle about how she had "fleshed up" in recent months. But they tried, and that's something.

It just goes to show, there's never a perfect time to welcome, but the effort to make someone more comfortable, as if they belong, is always rewarding, if difficult. And Katy did feel a certain gratification afterward, the kind you feel when you have stepped out of your comfort zone and served your fellow human being: "I was sorry when she came, but now it's over, I'm glad."

● GO FOR IT, EVEN IF YOU FEEL INSECURE ABOUT YOUR HOUSE: We can all relate to feeling as if our homes and spaces do not measure up. Too small. Too weedy. Too cluttered. Too, too, too! And also, not enough. Emily Webster of *Emily of Deep Valley* fame also had a big "too" about her abode: *Too old-fashioned.*

Emily lived with her elderly grandfather in a musty, dated home, of a vintage befitting the residence of a man who had fought at Gettysburg.

But now it was 1912, and the house was sorely lacking in modern innovations. She was embarrassed about any number of things, including the wax flowers in the parlor, which her awful crush mocked once upon seeing them. (Don't get us started on "Don." Oy.)

But she and her friends and cousin Annette were all graduating from high school, and there were many celebrations happening in people's homes. "There was a round of luncheons, teas and card parties for the girls who were going away." *Uff Da*, as they say in Minnesota. Would Emily contribute to this carousel of casual parties? After all, "She was too sensitive about her home to entertain often."

Emily worried that the other girls were serving such "novel refreshments," while she didn't have a clue about fashionable menus with party foods such as shrimp wiggle and marshmallow/pineapple fluff. Those other girls had mothers; she did not.

But ultimately, Emily decided not to let her "sensitivities" about her house rule the day. She "tried to shake such ideas out of her head," a heroine move right there. Emily went for it, cleaning like a maniac until that poky old house shone. She didn't attempt shrimp wiggle, but instead, wisely cooked foods she knew how to prepare well, using her late-mother's recipe for frog's legs. There was candlelight, and her grandmother's fine dishes, heavy silver, and damask tablecloth, and (interestingly) the entree was a hit. "...the frogs' legs...not only caused excitement and merriment but they were delicious as well." Emily's guests also dined on scalloped potatoes, garden vegetables, hot biscuits with homemade gooseberry preserves, and fresh peach pie.

The girls played lawn games, sang around the piano, and laughed their heads off. A good time was had by all, despite the mortifying wax flowers.

Brave Emily teaches us that when you park your "sensitivities" about your house, focus on the positive, and graciously open your imperfect space to others, people feel welcomed, and beautiful memories are made.

● WELCOME THE STRANGER AND FOREIGNER: Emily Webster also shows us how to live into the Bible's word for hospitality—*philoxenos:* love for the stranger or foreigner. Through her friendship with the Syrian immigrant community in Deep Valley, Emily is "renewed in hope," as writer Mitali Perkins puts it in her marvelous book, *Steeped in Stories: Timeless Children's Novels to Refresh Our Tired Souls.* Perkins, who immigrated from India as a child, saw herself in Emily and in the Syrian newcomers. "This connection between hospitality to the 'other' and a renewal of hope makes *Emily of Deep Valley* my favorite of Auntie Maud's stories," she writes. "As a young reader, I saw myself mirrored in Emily, as we all do. But I was also Yusef, Kalil, and Layla, longing for a warm American welcome."

● HOST YOUR OWN SUNDAY NIGHT LUNCH OR EQUIVALENT: A writer from British Columbia named Joelle Anthony read the Besty-Tacy books when she was younger. "All my life I wanted to have my own Sunday Night Lunch," she wrote. So she did, calling it Sunday Night Soup.

"We did want to take a page out of Betsy's book (pun intended) though and keep things very simple. That is how we came up with soup and bread…We wanted an event where our friends could be walking down the street and suddenly remember it's Sunday and just turn up our driveway and join us without worrying about contributing in any way… The benefits to Sunday Soup are immeasurable. We have made so many friends, so many connections."

● HOSPITALITY WHEN YOU (OR YOUR PANTRY) ARE RUNNING ON EMPTY: Hospitality looks different depending on our phase of life. The heroines would not want their example to make us feel that we are not "doing enough." We would do well to remember that there are seasons where we might be serving more than being served, and vice versa. A new mother tending to her baby, for instance, typically isn't going to have the capacity to throw a dinner party, whereas she may be more prone to drop-in visitors. An elderly person might have ample time to receive guests, but little energy to entertain them.

Sometimes these classic books can make casual hospitality look so effortless it seems impossible to us. But consider what was being served. If you dropped in at Francie Nolan's flat in Brooklyn, you would likely be treated to a cup of coffee, and maybe a slice of dry bread with a table-spoon of condensed milk. Heidi would share a wedge of grandfather's renowned homemade cheese. Sure, stock your pantry with tea and coffee, and the ingredients for your favorite throw-together treat, but our heroines teach us that the best thing to offer your guests is exactly what you have on hand. No matter how little that happens to be, served with a welcoming heart, it will be the perfect thing.

⬤ BE WILLING TO "IMPOSE": When we imagine ourselves dropping in unexpectedly at the Cuthbert house in Avonlea, or the Nolan flat in Brooklyn, or Heidi's grandfather's home in the Alps, our twenty-first century hearts are charmed by the idea that unexpected guests are . . . expected. And even more charmed that they are always welcome (or at least, made to feel so).

Between the invention of text messaging and our Western sensibil-ities that make us reluctant to impose, little room is left in our modern lives for the occasion of drop-in company. But let us look to one of our smallest heroines for an example of how we might rebrand *imposing*.

Heidi, our favorite young damsel traipsing about the mountainside with a gaggle of goats, was the Queen of Imposition.

Not only is her permanent arrival at her grandfather's house the last thing from "expected," this etiquette-unaware child loves to drop in on other unsuspecting villagers as well. Her favorite friend to drop in on is "the grandmother," as she called her dear friend Peter's blind and frail grandma. But the grandmother was blessed by her visit:

"Thank God, thank God!" the old woman said. "I hope she'll come again; she has done me so much good! What a soft heart she has, the darling, and how nicely she can talk."

Whereas Heidi's hardened grandfather always declined to enter the hut that was Peter's family home, Heidi had no such reluctance. And we see clearly the great benefit her presence is to the lonely old grandmother.

Take a note from our humble Heidi and consider being an "imposition" in someone's life in the near future. She prioritized surprising the grandmother with her presence because she "did not want to miss the chance to make the grandmother's heart joyful and light."

HEROINE CHALLENGE
SAY "YES," AND DON'T APOLOGIZE.

When our first internal response to unexpected guests is, "but my house isn't clean" or "the fridge is empty!", we inadvertently turn the focus onto ourselves—the opposite of a welcoming attitude. But this is merely a failure of imagination. And if there is one thing we readers are good at, it is imagining things differently from what they appear to be.

Is it possible to have a good conversation with a friend in a messy living room over a glass of lukewarm water? Why, yes, it is! With this assurance, free yourself to imagine the possibilities.

The next time you find yourself in those paralyzing minutes between the "hey, are you home?" text and the doorbell ringing (though they are rare, these occurrences are bound to happen occasionally!), ask yourself this: what is the goal of this visit? If the goal is to make your visitor feel loved and welcome, she doesn't need a clean house or freshly baked treat to feel those things. Sure, pick up the pillows and toss the toys into a bin, but while you are doing so, take a moment to put yourself in your friend's shoes. What has been going on in her life lately? What are her challenges? What might she be looking forward to? What do you admire most about your friend?

When the conditions of your home and pantry aren't perfect, commit instead to making sure your friend leaves your home refreshed by your encouraging words and sympathetic ear. Like Heidi, whenever you offer "joy and light," you are sharing a precious gift.

Jenny's Favorite Last-Minute Dutch Baby Pancake

This is one of my favorite go-to recipes for unexpected guests. The ingredients are all pantry staples, it's beautiful when it comes out of the oven, it's perfect for the morning or an afternoon snack, it pairs perfectly with coffee or tea, and it has a whimsical name to boot. It only takes about five minutes of prep time so you can throw it into the oven and vacuum the living room rug while it bakes for 25 minutes.

Ingredients

- 4 Tbsp. unsalted butter
- 3 large eggs
- ¾ C buttermilk*
- ¾ C flour
- ⅓ C sugar
- ¼ tsp. salt
- ¼ tsp. vanilla
- 1-2 C frozen or fresh berries
- Powdered sugar or maple syrup for serving

1. Preheat oven to 425 degrees F (218 C), slice butter into cubes and place in a large skillet (technically this recipe is designed for a 12" skillet, but I always use my 8" one with no problem) or Dutch oven without the lid.

2. Place skillet or Dutch oven in the oven (while preheating) to let the butter melt.

3. Meanwhile, whisk the eggs in a medium size bowl until foamy, add buttermilk, flour, sugar, salt, and vanilla, and blend until combined.

4. When butter is fully melted, swirl it around to cover the surface of the skillet/Dutch oven. Pour batter in skillet and scatter the berries on top.

5. Bake for 25 minutes or until pancake has puffed and is golden brown.

6. Remove from oven, sprinkle with powdered sugar or a drizzle of maple syrup and serve immediately.

Whisk in about a tablespoon of yogurt into whole milk as a substitute for buttermilk.

WHEN all pretenses are SET ASIDE, food AND decoration BECOME SOMETHING MUCH greater than THE sum OF THEIR PARTS: they become the BACKDROP THAT illuminates ALL the things WE LOVE ABOUT each other.

Chapter 4

PROFFER PUFFED SLEEVE HOSPITALITY LIKE A HEROINE

BEGUILE YOUR GUESTS WITH LUSTROUS TEA POURS AND ELEGANT COLD TONGUE

"Oh, dear, no! We must have cold tongue and chicken,
French chocolate and ice cream, besides."

AMY MARCH, *LITTLE WOMEN*

PROBLEM: You may feel like you are not quite up to more elaborate hosting, intimidated at the thought of throwing a cocktail party, tea party, or dinner party, never mind a ball at Pemberley with that smoldering Mr. Darcy lurking in the corners.

HEROINE SOLUTION: The heroines are full of tips on how to pull off the art of gathering with panache, confidence, and a sense of humor. In this chapter, you will gain confidence, ideas, and an enhanced community with your guests.

*I*F PINAFORE HOSPITALITY describes the conditions in which guests might be received (not perfect, casual, and spontaneous), Puffed Sleeve hospitality is the kind of entertaining that involves one's billowiest shoulder puffs as well as ambiance and conversation to match. Whereas Pinafore Hospitality is unplanned or at least unpretentious, Puffed Sleeve hospitality involves an invitation in advance, meal planning, and an air of refinement.

But does Puffed Sleeve Hospitality require a different set of skills than Pinafore Hospitality? Does one allow for more grace? Or is this only in our heads?

In a world that grows increasingly casual, we are here to defend, with the example of the heroines, the benefits of Puffed Sleeve Hospitality. The heroines prove that while Pinafore Hospitality offers ample opportunity to make guests feel loved and appreciated, Puffed Sleeve Hospitality has the potential to be what imaginative play is to children: an escape from reality that somehow brings us back into the real world feeling more...ourselves. Ah, how refreshing!

Puffed Sleeve Hospitality offers a moment to step out of the mundaneness of the everyday and forget for a few hours that we aren't sure how we will cover this month's rent, or that Gilbert may be getting ahead of us in school.

In the great Danish short story by Isak Dinesen, *Babette's Feast,* a mysterious French housekeeper who lives with two elderly Danish sisters wins the lottery in her home country and spends every penny on a celebratory meal for the sisters and ten of their guests.

The humble guests are accustomed to plain and unfussy fare, and despite being a close-knit religious community, many of them are nursing grudges or are otherwise not at peace with each other when they arrive. But the French feast Babette serves them is unlike anything they've ever encountered. The menu is of such grandeur and prepared with such meticulous attention that at first, they don't know how to act before such an offering.

Babette's feast transports them almost literally to heaven. By the time the feast draws to a close, they have accepted the great gift they've been given. Wrongs are made right, and they forgive one another with laughter and warm embraces. "The vain illusions of this earth had dissolved before their eyes like smoke, and they had seen the universe as it really is. They had been given one hour of the millennium . . . It was, to each of them, blissful to have become as a small child; it was also a blessed joke to watch old Brothers and Sisters, who had been taking themselves so seriously, in this kind of celestial second childhood."

The measure of Puffed Sleeve Hospitality is not an exotic menu, great fuss, or perfect execution, it is that your guests leave with a glow in their bosom and you as the hostess feel an ember from that same fire.

For most of us, Puffed Sleeve Hospitality is not sustainable on a daily basis, but this is also one of its greatest benefits. Puffed Sleeve Hospitality is a reminder that perfection is not necessary to our survival. All we need to have courage in this weary world is a small *taste*, and we will receive the refreshment a little extra care can bring.

A "PUFFED SLEEVE" NATURAL

"I'm just someone who likes cooking and for whom sharing food is a form of expression," Maya Angelou once said.

Queen Maya was a famously good hostess, treating friends and family and strangers alike to delectable food, aromatic ambience (before one dinner party, she burned lavender in a fire shovel, "which perfumed the entire space in an aromatic prelude to what was to come"), and "virtuoso" preparations in which she enthralled her guests before they popped one morsel into their mouths.

"Dr. Angelou (her preferred appellation) loved entertaining large groups or small," wrote one guest, Jessica B. Harris, in an article called "A Way With Words and a Spice Rack." "Her larder was always prepared for a party, and she was the kind of cook who knew just how to put things together, effortlessly entertaining with stories and tall tales while the cooking went on."

Sounds like Puffed Sleeve Hospitality to us, a heroine hosting a fancier gathering with panache, confidence, and a sense of humor. Notice we didn't say anything about the cost of the event. Besides some of Jane Austen's characters, most of our bookish leading ladies didn't preside over balls or expensive gatherings.

No, Puffed Sleeve Hospitality is all about the spirit of the host, who possesses a quality of elegance in her inviting, preparing, and executing a refined and generous assemblage of guests.

In this chapter, we will take a tour through the dining rooms, sitting rooms, parlors, and yes, ballrooms presided over by our heroines, gleaning insights from how they pulled off their poshest events, big and small. We will discuss the art of gathering—what makes for a tasteful and bountiful tea party, luncheon, dinner party, or special event? Read on as we convey some of the best heroine practices of extending an elegant, welcoming cordiality that money can't buy.

 ## An Avonlea Tea Party

There was something inside Anne of Green Gables that yearned for the finer things in life. Puffed sleeves! The rosebud spray tea set for company. Chicken salad—which was the very height of cultivated cuisine.

This poor, neglected waif in wincey arrived at Green Gables with a bundle of unmet desires of the heart. Many of these needs were eventually met by having good people care for her deeply. Even so, for years, she pined for "cups of glamour" as Lucy Maud Montgomery once wrote. One of the pivotal scenes in the book hinges on this desire of Anne's to be elegant, to proffer, in this case, some "puffed sleeve hospitality" to her bosom friend Diana Barry.

After Anne has lived at Green Gables for a few months, Marilla allows Anne to invite Diana over for tea, which electrifies her.

She begs for the rosebud tea set, but Marilla shuts that request down hard and fast. "Well, what next?" she asks, as if Anne had asked to have a unicorn perform at the tea party. Anne may use the old brown tea set only; however, Marilla offers some consolation prizes of cherry preserves, fruit cake, cookies, and snaps.

(This whole menu reinforces our belief that Marilla was running a secret bakery at Green Gables, as she always seemed to have a surplus of baked goods on hand at any given moment.)

Anne presses her luck again, requesting that she host this tea party in the parlor. Marilla, being Marilla, squashes that notion like a horsehair pillow. The girls can jolly well sit in the sitting room, which is for sitting. But another consolation prize follows, one that will lead to one of the most iconic scenes in the novel: Anne is told she may serve her guest from the half-full bottle of raspberry cordial, on the second shelf of the sitting room closet (whatever you say, Marilla).

Anne decides to make the best of things, despite having to pour from an old brown tea set and preside over her tea party in a boring sitting room. It's mind over matter, and in Anne's mind, she is a fancy lady hosting an elegant 'do.' Dignity, primness, and "toes in position" ensue, though we have no idea what position that is. Polite inquiries are made about each other's parents and guardians, including a query from Diana about Matthew Cuthbert's potato crops.

(If she could, Lorilee would now rhapsodize for six pages about Prince Edward Island potatoes. Let's just say she arranged every meal around whether or not potatoes—grown on the island in its signature, mineral-rich red dirt—could conceivably be a side dish. If you think, dear reader, that a potato is a potato, you have never tasted the scrummy spuds grown on Anne's beloved island.)

But back to the fancy tea party. After the girls loosen up and spend time in the orchard, gossiping and eating apples, they return to the house and some raspberry cordial, which is where the wheels come off (we will dive into this debacle in a future chapter).

For now, let us reflect that Anne's first attempt at Puffed Sleeve Hospitality was a bit of a bust. (If only Marilla had owned a label maker—what a different book this would be!)

But Anne definitely tried again and again to add a sprinkle of the special, a dollop of lavish, a dusting of deluxe, to her hosting opportunities, even if her puffed sleeve dreams had to fit within a pinafore reality—and budget.

She shows us that some of the most elegant gatherings can be accomplished on a shoestring. And as our next heroine's story reveals, lobster was a shoestring entrée back in the day.

Chicken Salad and Other Pined-For Luxuries

In *Little Women*, fancy-pants Amy March goes to great trouble to throw a luncheon party for the well-to-do girls in her drawing class. She dreams of serving them French chocolate, ice cream, and chicken, a most dashing dish. (Fascinatingly, lobster would have been cheap and abundant, but chicken was considered upscale because of the trouble it was to pluck the feathers.)

Amy also wanted to serve cold tongue, which was apparently the *de rigueur* thing for people to serve at a soiree such as Ms. March's "artistic fete."

"What do you want for lunch?" her mother asked. "Cake, sandwiches, fruit, and coffee will be all that is necessary, I suppose?" But in Amy's mind, that wasn't nearly showy enough for these la-di-da ladies.

"Oh, dear, no! We must have cold tongue and chicken, French chocolate and ice cream, besides," she says. "The girls are used to such things, and I want my lunch to be proper and elegant, though I do work for my living."

Little Women fans know that much of this little bash went sideways. Hannah's cooking didn't turn out well. Then the weather was so iffy that no one showed up, which presumably meant that they would all arrive on the next day, a prearranged "rain date." *Then* Amy ran into a rich boy on the omnibus (a large, horse drawn carriage used for public transportation), and she was humiliated when the lobster she bought escaped her basket—right in front of him!

(Is it not amazing that Amy was embarrassed about serving *lobster*? Public opinion about crustaceans has certainly risen in the last one-hundred and sixty years.)

"Oh horror!—the lobster, in all its vulgar size and brilliancy, was revealed to the highborn eyes of a Tudor!"

The lowly lobster ended up being the least of Amy's problems when one girl showed up, out of twelve. But the way the family March handled the ignominy was nothing less than pure refinement. (See more in heroine takeaways.)

REVEREND ALLEN AND WIFE ARE TREATED TO COLD TONGUE
(AND EVERYTHING ELSE IMAGINABLE)

Flipping the pages back to our girl Anne, she featured cold tongue on the menu of some of her most elevated hosting expeditions. Remember that time Reverend Allen and his wife came for "tea," and they ate absolutely everything under the sun? The menu included:

Baking-Powder Biscuits
Jellied Chicken

Cold Tongue
Red Jelly
Yellow Jelly
Whipped Cream
Lemon Pie
Cherry Pie
Three Kinds of Cookies
Fruit Cake
Yellow Plum Preserves
Pound Cake
Layer Cake
New Bread
Old Bread

(Presumably, the Avonlea First Responders had to be called upon to carry the poor, overstuffed Allens out the door on a pair of gurneys, even without taking into consideration the fact that Anne nearly poisoned them by accidentally baking Vicks VapoRub into her layer cake.)

And then again, in *Anne of the Island*, cold tongue secures a spot onto a frilly menu, this time on the occasion of Mrs. Douglas coming for "tea":

Cold Tongue
Chicken
Strawberry Preserves
Lemon Pie
Tarts
Chocolate Cake
Raisin Cookies
Pound Cake
Fruit Cake
Caramel Pie
Biscuits

WHEN PUFFED SLEEVE HOSPITALITY GOES HORRIBLY WRONG

In *Anne of Avonlea*, Anne and Diana prepare Green Gables for perhaps the puffiest sleeve occasion the house has ever hosted: the famous author Mrs. Morgan is in town and she's blessing the Cuthbert home with her presence at tea. Giddiness!

The vision of domestic transformation Maud paints for us fills the reader with anticipation: Green Gables is turned into an indoor garden as Anne and Diana adorn every surface of the tea table and its surroundings with bowers from the outdoors. Even Marilla, "who came in to criticize and remained to praise," was impressed.

Everything was perfect, from the weather to the menu to the appearance of the girls, who had chosen their most heroine-esque attire: white muslin. But alas, in this "chapter of accidents," Anne, Diana, and the other invited guests wait in vain for Mrs. Morgan and Priscilla to arrive.

The day ends in bitter disappointment and throbbing headaches for both girls. A letter from the post office retrieved that evening explains that Mrs. Morgan had a sprained ankle and could not leave her room.

While a telephone might have prevented the Particular Sorrows of this occasion, even with the invention of smartphones, our modern world is not cured of hospitality disappointments. But of course, in typical Maud fashion, this is not where the story ends. A comical conclusion awaits us.

Three chapters later, Mrs. Morgan (who is wearing tweed, not muslin), her niece, Priscilla (bedecked in silk), and the wife of a New York millionaire ("wonderfully gowned"), approach Green Gables unannounced, where they find Anne: not only *not* wearing muslin but covered in feathers from head to toe after changing out the ticking of a feather mattress. The bright red cherry on top of this hospitality nightmare is the bright red nose of Anne, who had that morning mistaken Marilla's red dye used for marking the patterns of rugs for freckle cream.

Here Anne is faced with a choice, and we are treated to an episode of quotidian heroism at its finest. Instead of turning her guests away, Anne invites them in, without acknowledging the terrible inconvenience of this spontaneous event, her ridiculous appearance, or her utter humiliation in meeting her literary idol in such a way.

Moments later, Diana serendipitously pops into the kitchen where Anne reveals her panic. "Diana Barry, who do you suppose is in that parlor at this very moment? Mrs. Charlotte E. Morgan...and a New York millionaire's wife...and here I am like *this*...and *not a thing in the house for dinner but a cold ham bone*, Diana!"

In the end, Mrs. Barry saves the day by providing Diana with a "nicely carved and jointed chicken" and hereby completes her penance for, years earlier, accusing Anne of intentionally intoxicating her daughter.

Despite everything, everyone at the table has a delightful afternoon. "Anne's hungry guests...did not seem to think anything was lacking and they ate the simple viands with apparent enjoyment."

After the guests leave, Anne declares to Diana, "'It has indeed been a feast of reason and flow of soul, hasn't it?...I believe we had a nicer time than if we'd known they were coming and been cumbered with much serving.'"

Maud teaches Anne and us that a true heroine is not at the mercy of her surroundings, however wonderful or lackluster they may be.

Puffed Sleeve Hospitality does not guarantee that guests become the best versions of themselves, just as Pinafore Hospitality does not mean that a casual gathering cannot lift spirits to great heights. Knowing the only thing you can control is your attitude, in hospitality as well as life, is the perfect blend of terrifying and empowering, isn't it?

On that note, let us raise our bubbling cups of courage and offer this toast: to rising above, whether Puffed or Pinafore, success or disaster.

HEROINE TAKEAWAYS

- **BE YOURSELF, EVEN IN FANCY SETTINGS:** Zora Neale Hurston knew how to be herself, even in a setting that would have intimidated most people. Once, at a literary awards dinner, Zora made a splash as she claimed four awards: a second-place fiction prize for her short story "Spunk," a second-place award in drama for her play *Color Struck*, and two honorable mentions.

"Lest anyone forget her," writes Valerie Boyd on the website Zora-nealehurston.com, "Hurston made a wholly memorable entrance at a party following the awards dinner. She strode into the room-jammed with writers and arts patrons, black and white-and flung a long, richly colored scarf around her neck with dramatic flourish as she bellowed a reminder of the title of her winning play: 'Coloooooor Struuckkkk!' Her exultant entrance literally stopped the party for a moment, just as she had intended. In this way, Hurston made it known that a bright and powerful presence had arrived."

- **DECORATE WITH "FLUMMERY":** Re: Reverend Allen and Wife Eat Absolutely Everything at a Frilly Green Gables Luncheon: Anne wanted to decorate the table with ferns and wild roses, enhancing the staggering spread of food on the table with natural beauty.

"I think that's all nonsense," sniffed Marilla. "In my opinion it's the eatables that matter, not flummery decorations." Well, Ms. Cuthbert, we disagree with you here, but first we must look up "flummery."

1. empty compliments; nonsense. Foolish humbug.

2. a sweet dish made with beaten eggs, milk, sugar, and flavorings.

Obviously, Marilla had in mind the first definition; she thought decorating the table was superfluous. But we don't, and neither did Anne. That girl was all about the spiffy, beautifying little extras. Ferns and wild roses would have been gorgeous, and they are the perfect example to illustrate that flummery doesn't have to cost much, or anything! For Lorilee's son's wedding reception, a post-Covid picnic in the park, she collected silverware for a hundred people at thrift stores, bundling the forks and knives with ribbons. The picnic tables were covered in creamy thrift store tablecloths, with one antique pitcher or canning jar adorning each table, and hydrangeas from her neighbor Nancy's stunning garden plopped in each vase. There were donuts with candy-colored frosting for dessert, presented on cake plates and cupcake stands of various heights, and jazz music playing on the sound system.

Flummery? You bet your bottom donut, but also resplendent, too, and deluxe on a dime.

● ELEGANCE IS AS ELEGANCE DOES: In Gwendolyn Brooks's 1960 poem "The Bean Eaters," she reveals two people who love each other, eating a humble meal in their rented room.

> *"They eat beans mostly, this old yellow pair.*
> *Dinner is a casual affair.*
> *Plain chipware on a plain and creaking wood,*
> *Tin flatware."*

The "puffed sleeve" element here is not how snazzy the food is or how impressive the setting, but in their unwavering commitment to each other and how they revel in their stories and memories. "And remembering...Remembering, with twinklings and twinges."

We have a feeling that these "Bean Eaters" possessed a hospitable spirit. The beauty of their lives and a deep shared love strikes us as nothing short of elegant.

- HOLD YOUR HEAD HIGH WHEN ONE PERSON SHOWS UP: We've already deconstructed Amy's debacle of a luncheon, featuring an overblown and budget-straining menu, a runaway lobster, and a bevy of guests too snooty to show up, but let's just take a moment and think how we would feel if we invited a dozen people to our house for a meal, and just one person—Miss Eliott—showed up. Embarrassed, we would guess. Also, sad and probably rejected. Yet somehow Amy held her head high as she welcomed her solitary guest.

"In came Amy, quite calm and delightfully cordial to the one guest who had kept her promise. The rest of the family, being of a dramatic turn, played their parts equally well, and Miss Eliott found them a most hilarious set... The remodeled lunch being gaily partaken of."

We'd like to tip our lobster forks in salute to a heroine who kept her wits about her in a humiliating situation. Of course, she never should have burned Jo's manuscript. We are still mad at her for that. But she showed us all how to keep calm and carry on, even when one person shows up at your party.

HEROINE CHALLENGE
BRING YOUR OWN VERSION OF "FANCY"

It's not the first time we've said it, but it can't be emphasized enough: the best way to make others feel at home is to *be yourself*. The next time you host a Puffed Sleeve event, large or small, think of all the typical ways of elevating that particular occasion (a special cocktail, carefully crafted floral arrangements, exotic Hors d'oeuvres, etc.), and if none of them invokes your creative spark, take a note from Cassie's mama and Zora and forget them all.

(continues on next page)

Instead, start by asking yourself: what do I love that I can naturally use to inspire my guests? Is there a particular color palette that makes your heart sing, a simple but delicious dish you've been eating nonstop that you could serve in small ramekins as appetizers, or a wildflower that grows profusely in your backyard that you could use as a table centerpiece?

My mom (Jenny's) is particularly good at this kind of naturally elevated hospitality. She is far more likely to serve you stovetop popcorn cooked in ghee, a sauteed vegetable from her garden in a pool of melted butter, or a bite of imported cheese she's just discovered, than caviar or any number of arduously assembled trifles. And yet, dinner at her house is always as unpretentious as it is special. When you serve what you love, and not what you think will impress, guests are put at ease. They are assured that behind all the preparation is not a display of extravagance, but an earnest desire to share.

When all pretense of fanciness is eliminated, food and decoration melt away into matters of little consequence. As in *Babette's Feast*, they become something much greater than the sum of their parts: they become the backdrop that illuminates all the things we love about each other.

Lorilee's Crazy Easy, Budget-Friendly, Fancy Slow Cooker Red Wine-Soaked Pears

Note: This will make your house smell like a winery, and the alcohol *does not cook off*, but it's so fun (especially the part where you stand there and empty an entire bottle into your slow cooker—oddly hypnotic and calming, and fancy, yet inexpensive and effortless.

Ingredients

2 (29-oz.) cans pear halves

1 (750-ml.) bottle drinkable yet cheap red wine

1 C white sugar

1 tsp. vanilla extract

1 cinnamon stick

2 star anise (optional)

6 Tbsp. sweetened whipped cream (for garnish, after cooking)

(continues on next page)

INSTRUCTIONS

1. Use a 6-quart slow cooker.

2. Drain pears and plop them into your slow cooker (it makes a fun sound).

3. Add the entire bottle of wine (more fun sounds: glug, glug, glug!).

4. Stir in the sugar a bit gingerly.

5. Add vanilla and float the cinnamon stick and star anise on top.

6. Cover and cook on low for 5 hours, or on high for about 2.

7. Serve warm in bowls with a large dollop of whipped cream.

What ideas would you like to implement at your next hosted event?

....
....
....
....
....
....
....
....
....
....
....
....
....
....
....
....
....

HEIDI'S TOASTED CHEESE

MRS. SOWERBY'S currant BUNS

MEG MURRY'S MIDNIGHT HOT COCOA

CASSIE LOGAN'S ROASTED PEANUTS

Cozy offerings

JANE Eyre
Charlotte Brontë

BY THE FIRE

HANNAH'S TURNOVERS

KRISTIN LAVRANSDATTER'S PORRIDGE

MAYA'S MOTHER'S 2:30AM BISCUITS

Chapter 5

COZY LIKE A HEROINE

Butter Buns by the Fire and Other Ways to Get Snug, Warm and Comfy

"The homey sounds and scents cushioned me."

MAYA ANGELOU

PROBLEM: You are stressed, anxious, and too hard on yourself. You know you should take time out for self-care, but what does that even mean, and how can you make it a priority with everything else going on in your life? How can food be part of the solution, not the problem?

HEROINE SOLUTION: The heroines provide ample proof that coziness, rest, and self-compassion are not luxuries, they are a necessary tonic to our overextended lives. They show us how food can be a part of a cozy life that includes plenty of soothing, comforting, and stress-relieving "cushion time."

*I*n *I Know Why the Caged Bird Sings,* Maya Angelou paints an inviting portrait of coziness, describing how she read a beloved book before the fire as her Mama fried corn cakes for supper.

"Pots rattled in the kitchen where Momma was frying corn cakes to go with vegetable soup for supper, and the homey sounds and scents cushioned me as I read of Jane Eyre in the cold English mansion of a colder English gentleman. Uncle Willie was engrossed in the Almanac, his nightly reading, and my brother was far away on a raft on the Mississippi."

The homey sounds and scents cushioned me...We aspire to this state of being, cocooned by the sounds of someone preparing food, and by the delicious aromas of butter, sweetness, and cakiness. And we love that every member of the family—except for Momma, the chef—was enveloped in a good book.

We admire the way Maya chose the word "cushioned" to describe her emotional condition, as the warmth and coziness she was experiencing went deeper than just a mellow moment before dinner. "Cushioned" evokes a sense of softening, absorbing the hard edges, of shelter and protection. The cold winds of stress, hardship, and pain may have blown all around this little girl, but inside Momma's kitchen was a quality of deep coziness that took the edge off of Maya's troubles. She was safe, warm, and cared for, and the goodness of fried corn bread helped her lean into all that was comforting, kindly, and tender in her life.

The opposite of cushioned is to be exposed, unprotected from the harsh elements. The heroines teach us that stress and harshness can be offset by intentional "cushioning," helping each one of *us* lean into all that is comforting, kindly, and tender in *our* lives.

Call it self-care or cushioning, just don't diminish how important it is to find coziness on a regular basis. Rest and self-compassion are not luxuries; they are a necessary tonic to our overextended lives.

Maya joins other heroines across genres and centuries who adored nothing more than butter buns by the fire (Jane Austen and company), toasting cheese by the fire (Heidi), and roasting peanuts on the fire (Cassie Logan). Our heroines were wild about fireside meals and snacks, and could hygge with the best of them, especially Queens of Cozy, Beth March and Jane Austen, who famously wrote "There is nothing like staying at home for real comfort."

COZY: AMERICAN HEROINE BETH MARCH 🌼

"Beth is like a warm, rosy lamp—a cozy presence that makes a house a home," write the authors of *The Little Women Cookbook*, Jenne Bergstrom and Miko Osada.

Our heroine Beth March is a cushioning presence in her family, a girl of quiet strength and a servant's soul. Her parents and her three sisters, Meg, Jo, and Amy, are the center of her world, a world she softens and graces with her sweetness and genius at homemaking.

In chapter one of *Little Women*, as the girls discuss who will give what presents to Marmee, Beth remembers how shy she used to feel when it was her birthday, and everyone watched her open her presents. "'It was dreadful to have you sit looking at me while I opened the bundles,' said Beth, who was toasting her face and the bread for tea at the same time."

Ooh, snug as a bug in a rug—that was our Beth, especially if she was also wrapped up in a homemade quilt while she made grilled cheese (we are guessing) over an open fire. She knew how to capture a comfy moment.

Beth spent what energy she had on making her home a haven for all. "She was a housewifely little creature, and helped Hannah keep home neat and comfortable for the workers."

Later in the book, Beth offers the only actual recipe in the book, for golden butternut squash. This recipe is featured in an edition of the girls' homestyle newsletter, *The Pickwick Portfolio*, within an article called "the History of Squash," written by and starring Beth. Following some preamble about the history of squash, Beth enters the scene: "...a little girl, in a brown hat and blue dress, with a round face and snub nose, went and bought (the squash) for her mother. She lugged it home, cut it up and boiled it in the big pot; mashed some of it, with salt and butter, for dinner; and to the rest she added a pint of milk, two eggs, four spoons of sugar, nutmeg and some crackers; put it in a deep dish and baked it till it was brown and nice; and the next day it was eaten by a family named March."

(Delicious, and so heartening on a cold winter's day! We must try this recipe just exactly as it is, don't you think?)

Did Beth ever know how much her adoring family relied on her for comfort and support? No wonder we all weep every single time we reread this book. Restful Beth drew strength from her cozy life, and that bone-deep warmth melted the hearts of all who knew her.

Alcott writes, "There are many Beths in the world, shy and quiet, sitting in corners till needed, and living for others…cheerfully."

Do you know a Beth? A gentle homebody who craves comfort and snugness? "The Beths of today would rather stay in for popcorn and board games than go out to the hipster gastropub," write Bergstrom and Osada. "Our Beths are cheerful bearers of emotional labor, who will make you macaroni and cheese and brownies if you are having a bad day, and show up with a thermos of chicken soup when you are under the weather. Comfort food is their specialty…"

In other words, Beth was a Cushion, and boy, do we need cushions in our lives.

"Cosy": British Heroine Jane Austen

"When I'm not cooking, eating or writing about food, I like to read," writes Jean of the *Delightful Repast* blog. "There's nothing so delightful to me as a rainy day at home, in my robe, with tea and buns (or scones or crumpets) and a good book (preferably English)….A day spent in Jane Austen's world can be a marvelous restorative."

On Janeaustenworld.com, Jean offers a recipe for Sally Lunn buns, or Bath Buns—hot, buttery buns made with flour, milk, butter, and caraway seeds, and frosted with a milky sweet glaze, a cozy gem of Regency teatime. Jane referred to them herself once in an 1801 letter to her sister, Cassandra. Staying with a cranky aunt, she joked to her sister that she would make herself a cheap guest by "disordering my Stomach with Bath bunns."

English muffins were also a comfy staple among Jane and her characters. Who can forget that Nervous Nellie Mr. Woodhouse gently rebuking Emma for passing the muffins twice? The man had some issues, to be sure, but likely he was influenced by the prevalent thought that muffins were indigestible. Perpetuating hyperacidity? Why, it was not to be abided! "There is nobody half as attentive and civil as you are," he says to Emma as they debriefed the previous evening's tea with guests. "If any thing, you are too attentive. The muffin last night—if it had been handed round once, I think it would have been enough." Speak for yourself, Mr. Woodhouse. We would certainly like to be offered muffins more than once, especially if they are slathered with creamy butter.

According to Pen Vogler, in her marvelous little book *Tea with Jane Austen*, Emma's muffins would have been "toasted front to back (not in the middle) and pulled (not cut) apart around the waist."

Martha Lloyd, who lived with Jane and her family for years at Chawton Cottage, authored the *Martha Lloyd Household Book*, a trove of recipes and remedies. She and Jane were so close Jane described her as a sister. Her recipe for toasted cheese calls for the home cook to "grate the Cheese & add to it one egg, & a teaspoonful of Mustard, & a Little Butter." Jane herself appreciated toasted cheese, praising in a letter a friend's hospitality during her visit: "It is impossible to do justice to the hospitality of his attentions towards me; he made a point of ordering toasted cheese for supper entirely on my account."

Like Beth March, Jane would have totally toasted her face by the fire, nestled in front of the hearth by herself or her loved ones. "For a cosy fireside tea, people would toast and lavish butter on…'butter buns,'" said Vogler. "…The cookery writer Mrs. Rundell suggests flavoring them with nutmeg, Jamaica peppers (allspice), caraway, or rose water."

Vogler includes a recipe for butter buns from *Martha Lloyd's Household Book*; it includes what we believe to be the cuddliest ingredient of all heroine recipes: currants! Not only do many of the Regency teatime recipes call for the dried, dark purple berries, but the ingredient prevailed into the Victorian era and beyond. According to Amy Cotler, the author of *The Secret Garden Cookbook*, "cozy currant buns" were the snuggest of snacks.

"Lightly spiced buns, often sweetened with dried currants, became popular in England during the Tudor period," she writes, noting that these buns were best enjoyed "still warm from the cottage chimney oven and accompanied by milk."

A COZY MESS OF CORNMEAL DUMPLINGS

There is so much cozy food in Zora's *Their Eyes Were Watching God*, including soda crackers with cheese, lemonade sweetened with ribbon cane syrup, and fried chicken and macaroni.

One thing we admire about Janie Mae Crawford, the book's heroine, was how she grew to believe that she was worthy of peace, comfort, pleasure, and being loved. She persisted until she had sweet things in her life, including Tea Cake, her great love, a handsome man fifteen years her junior, whose very name refers to a crispy, chewy circle of sugary dough.

Before Tea Cake arrives on the scene, Janie knows how to comfort others, even leaving her first husband (an elderly man who treated her like a pack mule) *after* frying him a hoe cake to go with his coffee. "She dumped the dough on the skillet and smoothed it over with her hand. She wasn't even angry," Hurston writes.

Her second husband, Jodi, regarded her as his possession to control, a trophy instead of a human being. When Jodi died, Janie was finally ready for Tea Cake, with whom she felt safe and secure. They even ate warm, homestyle food together as part of their comfy lifestyle.

When it came to fresh caught fish, Tea Cake was clear: "Ah'll clean 'em, you fry 'em and let's eat. They went out into the kitchen and fixed up the hot fish and corn muffins and ate. Then Tea Cake went to the piano without so much as asking and began playing blues and singing, and throwing grins over his shoulder. The sounds lulled Janie to soft slumber and she woke up with Tea Cake combing her hair…It made her more comfortable and drowsy."

Janie even used comfy foods in her metaphors. When townsfolk criticized her for loving Tea Cake, she shot back. "Now they got to look in to me loving Tea Cake and see if it was done right or not! They don't know if life is a mess of cornmeal dumplings and if love is a bed quilt!"

We like the idea of life being like a mess of cornmeal dumplings—heartening, tender, and full of assurances that home is where the heart is.

KRISTIN LAVRANSDATTER, SIGRID UNDSET, AND THE SCANDINAVIAN OBSESSION WITH COZINESS

Kristin Lavransdatter, the gripping trilogy by Sigrid Undset (winner of the 1928 Nobel Prize for Literature), takes place in the author's native country of Norway. Set in the Middle Ages, it is the perfect series to fall into in the winter months, wrapped in a handmade quilt. Even better if it's near a toasty fire with a view of falling snow.

In Denmark, Norway's southerly neighbor, this type of coziness is referred to as *hygge*, a term we Americans have become familiar with in recent years as we try to adopt this element of Danish lifestyle into our own. But there's a similar but not-quite-equivalent Norwegian term, *koselig*, that feels more fitting when talking about Kristin.

Whereas *hygge* is about creating coziness within frigid conditions, *koselig* is not retreating from the cold of winter, but rather, bundling up in warm clothing and facing the elements as a group and finding warmth in the togetherness. *Koselig*, as Jason Wilson writes in an article for *Readers Digest*, is "celebrating what winter is, instead of longing for all the things it isn't."

This is a fitting metaphor for our heroine Kristin, who must find a way to confront her sometimes chilling earthly and spiritual trials and reconcile them with the true source of her inner peace. She must face the mistakes of her youth and find the hope that was there all along.

Porridge is a big theme in the trilogy. Perhaps not a theme covered in college literature courses, we hereby deem it a highly effective literary device for creating a setting of coziness.

In Kristin's story, we read of breakfast porridge, dinner porridge, porridge with mead and beer, porridge served on a "fine wooden platter," and porridge cooked for such a sizable crowd that it must be made in a cauldron. While the simply seasoned fare of these novels (also mentioned: boiled meats and barley bread) may not leave us smacking our lips, porridge is the epitome of inner warmth and filling food.

In an article speaking about the harsh Norwegian winters, David G. Allan writes this about the mindset of *koselig*, "Darkness and isolation can be celebrated because they provide the need for their relief. The act of creating our own light and warmth produces peace and contentment." He is describing exactly the "heroine mindset," whether he knows it or not.

MEG MURRY'S DARK AND STORMY NIGHT, MAYA'S AND BAILEY'S 2:30 AM PARTY, AND THE SHELTERING PROMISE OF A FLICKERING FLAME

There is nothing like surrounding darkness to reinforce the coziness of a warm fire or burning stove. Whether it is Heidi and her grandfather toasting cheese over an open flame as dusk is falling or the Ingalls family eating cornbread and beans around the campfire under the stars, darkness implies such mystery and unknown that even the small glow of a candle flame can set our hearts at ease.

We're struggling to think of a cozier opening line than Madeleine L'Engle's, *A Wrinkle in Time*: "It was a dark and stormy night." We meet Meg Murry sitting on her bed in her attic bedroom, fearful of an approaching hurricane, reliving her awful day at school, and just generally ruminating over the tragedy of her misfitted-ness.

But she decides that hot chocolate will cheer her up, and upon entering the kitchen, where "The furnace purred like a great, sleepy animal," sees that a light is on and her little brother, Charles Wallace, is waiting for her. He has already started a pot of milk to warm on the stove, and Meg marvels at this small child's ability to probe her mind with "frightening accuracy."

Soon, Meg's mother joins them, and Meg is greatly bolstered by the soft glow of her mother's words of comfort and her brother's unwavering support, even as she is surrounded by the darkness of her (very real) teenage problems.

Maya Angelou too, in *I Know Why the Caged Bird Sings*, is another heroine who finds love in the midst of darkness, metaphorically and literally. She recalls the time when she was awoken by her mother to come downstairs to the kitchen in the middle of the night. Like Meg, she finds her brother waiting for her. The clock on the table reads 2:30, and Maya's mother says, "I am giving a party and you are my honored and only guests." As they are served crispy brown biscuits and warm milk chocolate around the stove, Maya says, "there was nothing for it but to laugh at our beautiful and wild mother."

"GRUMPY" IS NOT A FLAVOR, AND COZY IS AN OFFERING

The March household in *Little Women* included Hannah, the kindly housekeeper and cook who treats her profession with the sacred duty of a nurse: choosing food and drink for her four little cherubs based on their physical, mental, and spiritual conditions. Yes, Mr. March was away at war and dearly missed, but a Marmee *and* a Hannah? How could Meg complain about not being "like other girls" when other girls might not have had either?

We may have modern conveniences, but the cozy setting in which we find four disgruntled sisters in chapter four is enviable despite the palpable dissatisfaction (an attitude which eventually changes. These are heroines we speak of, after all).

In the midst of the morning bickering that opens the chapter, Hannah walks into the room and lays two piping hot turnovers onto the table for Meg and Jo, who are about to begin their cold walk to jobs they both loathe.

"These turnovers were an institution, and the girls called them 'muffs', for they had no others and found the hot pies very comforting to their hands on cold mornings. Hannah never forgot to make them, no matter how busy or grumpy she might be, for the walk was long and bleak. The poor things got no other lunch and were seldom home before two."

While turnovers solve a lot of problems, they admittedly don't solve *all* problems. But as readers, we have the perfect opportunity here to take a couple steps to the right, curve our torsos, tilt our heads, and look at Cozy a little differently. Just at the moment when Meg feels the weight of another day looking after four ungrateful children, and Jo the long hours attending to her grouchy aunt's tiresome requests, *two turnovers appear on the table.*

If the March sisters failed to recognize the warmth and luxury emanating from this scene, we, the reader, have received the gift of sight. We learn from quiet Hannah (whose name comes from the Hebrew word for "favor" or "grace"), that cozy is an offering, capable of lessening the harshest winter chill. Coziness is a gift you can give even when you wake up on the wrong side of the bed. However grumpy Hannah might have been that morning, it had no bearing on the flavor of those turnovers.

Assuming you don't actually have someone baking you steaming pastry pockets of sweet or savory fillings for your commute to work, the question of "Who is warming your hands with baked goods so that you might have the courage to face the coldness of the world?" is a metaphorical one. How can we thank our Hannah's and help them feel seen?

And if we tilt our heads in the other direction, we might ask ourselves, is there someone in our own lives for whom *we* could be a Hannah?

HEROINE TAKEAWAYS

⬤ NURTURING MOMENTS BUILD STRENGTH: "In the heart of the house, where we had gathered after supper," Cassie Logan and her family, including her parents, siblings, grandmother, and uncle, leaned into a nurturing moment that would cushion them all, even from painful stories and current realities.

"...in the fireplace itself, in a black pan set on a high wire rack, peanuts roasted over the hickory fire as the waning light of day swiftly deepened into a fine velvet night speckled with white forerunners of a coming snow, and the warm sound of husky voices and rising laughter mingled in tales of sorrow and happiness and days past but not forgotten."

We bask in this scene which appeals to all the senses—the sight of a fine velvet night, speckled with snow, the warming touch of the hickory fire, the sound of beloved voices telling stories, the smell and taste of roasting peanuts. Cassie faces many traumatic things in her young life, but it is moments like these that give us hope. We know that in each care-full and comforting moment, Cassie is building the resilience and strength she needs to be the heroine of her life, not the victim. When we lean into nurturing moments "in the heart of the house," we tend to see ourselves in a way that promotes growth and security.

Perhaps you have heard of the term "glimmer," which refers to experiences, sensations, or comforting moments that "cue safety." A glimmer is the opposite of a trigger, and "is something that helps us connect with a sense of our felt safety and step back into our window of tolerance," writes therapist Aundi Kolber in her book *Strong Like Water: Finding the Freedom, Safety and Compassion to Move Through Hard Things—and Experience True Flourishing*. "I love the language of glimmer because it literally speaks to lighting up a vital part of ourselves that makes us human."

Like Cassie, we can resource our souls with glimmers, lighting the way to deepened security, healing, and strength.

● A COMFORTING MEAL REASSURES AND SOOTHES, NO MATTER THE BUDGET: Is there a more sustaining soul in all of heroine literature than Dickon's worthy mother, Susan Sowerby? We meet Susan in *A Secret Garden* by Frances Hodgson Burnett, and admire her ability to care well for fourteen children, including Dickon and Martha, friends of the orphaned and privileged Mary Lennox. A Yorkshire cottager, Susan lives in a homely four-bedroom cottage that, according to Amy Cotler, dated back "as much as a thousand years," and was the traditional home of "people who were servants to the Lord of the manor," in this case, Mary's uncle. While we don't want to glorify the hardships and hunger of the cottagers, we admire Susan's capacity to nurture her children and even Mary, a child of the manor, with nourishing foods such as a rustic cottage loaf. "I'll tell thee what, lad," Mrs. Sowerby said to her son, referring to Mary and Colin, her invalid cousin. "When tha goes to 'em in the mornin' tha' shall take a pail o' good new milk an I'll bake 'em a crusty cottage loaf or some buns wi' currants in 'em, same as you children like."

Provisioning a family that size would have challenged the most gifted of cooks, but Mrs. Sowerby rose to the challenge, growing fruits and vegetables, and preserving whatever would keep well over the winter. Dickon, who could coax a potato—or a "tattie"—out of a rock, it seems, helped his mother keep the family fed, even in late winter, "the hungriest months," according to Cotler, when cottagers would run dangerously low on stored food. "During the cold months the iron pot that hung over the hearth bubbled with whatever was on hand: tattie broth, pease porridge, or winter vegetable stew." In her recipe for tattie broth, Cotler calls for butter or bacon drippings, an onion, water or chicken broth, a carrot, and maybe cabbage and turnips. Picture the Sowerby clan, gathered around the hearth, sipping at their bowls of warm, filling tattie broth. We feel cozier already, just imagining it. What Susan Sowerby lacked in worldly goods she more than made up for in resourcefulness and warmth. She is truly a portrait of how to cozy like a heroine—no matter one's budget.

HEROINE CHALLENGE
BUILD IN A *HYGGE* ROUTINE

According to Bronte Aurell, Danish entrepreneur and cookbook author, "Hygge" [pronounced "hyoo-guh"] refers to the warm, happy feeling you get when you are surrounded by lovely people you care about. To hygge, you need hyggelige things around you—blankets, candles, comfort food, an open fire, or whatever else makes you feel all cozy and warm inside." (By the way, we don't think it is a coincidence that her first name is *Bronte*, do you?)

(continues on next page)

The idea of hygge is that it is not a kind of self-care you schedule or "make time for," but rather, a coziness that fits effortlessly into your lifestyle. Think about the mundane or ordinary parts of your day and imagine how you might make them a little cozier, for yourself or others.

Candles are my (Jenny's) favorite way to elevate routine moments. I love to light a beeswax candle while I drink my morning coffee, or even while I'm cleaning up the kitchen in the evening! Another favorite hygge habit in our home is to have a puzzle going on the dining room table. If someone lingers there on her way between two rooms, there's a good chance someone will join her, and a good chance the kettle will be whistling a few minutes later.

Recipe

MAYA ANGELOU'S BUTTERMILK BISCUITS

INGREDIENTS

4 C flour

½ tsp. salt

2 Tbsp. baking powder

1 tsp. baking soda

1 C lard or butter

2 C buttermilk

INSTRUCTIONS

1. Preheat oven to 375 degrees F (190 C).
2. Sift dry ingredients into large bowl.
3. Cut in lard.
4. Mix in buttermilk.
5. Turn out onto bench floured counter.
6. Roll out to ½ inch thick.
7. Dip 2-inch water glass in flour.
8. Cut out biscuits.
9. Bake 20 minutes on ungreased cookie sheet until golden brown.
10. Serve warm with butter and jam (Might we recommend black currant? If you can find it).

"We cannot TRULY
nourish OTHERS, AND BE
NOURISHED ourselves,
without CONNECTEDNESS:
TO THE Land, to
the SEASONS, and MOST
IMPORTANTLY, to each
other.

Chapter 6

NOURISH LIKE A HEROINE

FEED AND NURTURE YOURSELF AND YOUR LOVES WITH DEVOTION, IMAGINATION, AND WHOLESOMENESS

"...'Come for dinner' is more than just an invitation to a meal; it's a celebration of community. Dinner nourishes our bodies, but it's the connection with people we love that nourishes our souls, and that's what I actually crave the most."

INA GARTEN

PROBLEM: You don't feel that you have the time, energy, or skill to nourish yourself and your family, so you resort too often to fast food and prepackaged food, which leads you to feel guilty and inadequate. You may forget that food is not something to be feared, dread the scale, or fret about the amount of time it takes to prep, cook, and clean up afterward.

HEROINE SOLUTIONS: Our heroines remind us again and again that the primary goal of food is to nourish. Yet nourishing yourself and your family well doesn't mean you have to be a chef all the time. Learning a few basic skills—how to meal plan like Meg March, for example—and stocking a pantry well can make all the difference in being able to cook more wholesome, nourishing meals. Meg, Maya, and company bring us back around to the joyful idea that food is on our side.

"FOOD IS A KIND OF LOVE YOU CAN SEE," writes cookbook author Wini Moranville, and for the heroines, feeding and nurturing those they loved was a matter of vital importance. Take Meg March. In *Little Women*, she works through every recipe in *The Young Housekeeper's Friend*—a popular cookbook of her day. Or Katy Carr, who, as a bed-ridden young teenager, planned family meals, only to eventually drive her housekeeper to drink (we are pretty sure it happened).

In this chapter, we explore the two sides of the nourish/nurture coin, feeding ourselves and our loves with care and panache. How can we create a repast which turns out so well, it becomes, like Maya Angelou wrote about her grandmother's fried ham and biscuit breakfasts, "a meal to make any Sunday proud?"

But first, let's discuss feeding our spirits as well as our bodies, and how the two go together.

WHAT NOURISHES OUR SOULS

In her pre-Covid book, *The Rabbit Effect: Live Longer, Happier, and Healthier with the Groundbreaking Science of Kindness*, Dr. Kelli Harding demonstrates the social factors that play a major role in our health. "There's a social dimension to health that we've completely over-looked in our scramble to find the best and most cutting-edge medical care…Ultimately, what affects our health in the most meaningful ways has as much to do with how we treat one another, how we live, and how we think about what it means to be human than with anything that happens in the doctor's office."

The heroines seemed to understand this idea of nourishing mind, body, and soul intuitively. When Janie Crawford in *Their Eyes Were Watching God* is isolated by the bitter gossip in her hometown, her one friend, Pheoby brings over a "heaping plate of mulatto rice," (rice made with crispy bacon, onions, and tomatoes) and sits with her for a while. In *Little Women*, the March women tend to their immigrant neighbors in their time of need. And in *Emma*, Emma Woodhouse makes "charitable visits" to poor and sick members of her community. There is an understanding that being alone is different from feeling disconnected, and the latter is a dangerous thing.

The secret to nourishing and flourishing, according to the heroines, is hidden in plain sight. We cannot truly nourish others, and be nourished ourselves, without connectedness: to the land, to the seasons, and most importantly, to each other.

The heroines agree: eating nourishes the body and being together nourishes the soul. Doing both together is cause for celebration every time.

FEASTING WITHOUT FEAR

The idea that healthy eating might look like eating chia seeds on a bed of kale in front of a screen, alone, had not been invented in the time of our heroines. You might have eaten alone if you were traveling. But for the most part, eating sandwiched slices of processed meats with a gentle coating of chemical preservatives in your cubicle while finishing your spreadsheets was yet the stuff of futuristic nightmares.

The delightful thing about reading about food in our heroine novels is the idea that food is the means by which our souls and bodies are *nourished,* as opposed to *punished*. We won't ever find the secret stash of

diet books hidden under one of Marilla's twelve pies in her gluten-ro-
bust pantry, because it doesn't exist. Our heroines were not eating broth
and celery sticks between carb-laden meals; they seemed to feast with
abandon. Was this feasting merely the fantasy of fiction?

But here, we find the truth to be "more true" in fiction. It is in fictional eating where we actually have a chance to come to our senses
about the true nature of "calories." As Robert Farrar Capon says in his
wonderfully soul-nourishing book, *The Supper of the Lamb*, "A calorie is
not a thing; it is a measurement. In itself, it does not exist...no one ever
yet got his teeth sunk into a calorie." He goes on to say, "How sad, then,
to see real beings...living their lives in abject terror of things that do not
even go bump in the night." Isn't it true that when we read of the feasting
at Anne's Sunday school picnic, or of bountiful hindquarters of pork in
Emma, *that* is when we remember that it is *the calorie* that is fictional,
not eating without fear?

It's not that the sometimes unwanted effects of calories are not real,
it's just that they tend to take precedence over all the other *good* side
effects of eating in our current cultural discussions of food. The heroines show us that being connected to the land, the seasons, and to each
other is a natural protection against the fear of The Calorie.

If we were dependent on what is currently available to us according
to the season, and if we ate with fervor and joy when in the company
of others, our gratitude for delicious food and good company would
naturally triumph over our fear of increasing poundage.

THE BENEFITS OF FEASTING & FASTING

But what else? Are there any health benefits to eating in a more connected way? Modern science says what the heroines already know: yes.

A person can survive on root vegetables and a little water. We
know this. And yet, we feel the longing of the Ingalls family in the
core of our being when we read *The Long Winter*. We know that mere

survival can portend starvation, a very real possibility for Laura and her family. The relief we feel when this family finally gets a full meal is palpable, emanating off the pages and flooding our own inner corners of emptiness.

For most of us, true hunger is not a pending threat, and we (hopefully) don't take that for granted. But if there is a downside to ever-available abundance, it is the bigger possibility that we could forget the lessons that come with Not Enough.

Here's another heroine example of "going without" that happened naturally for some of our heroines. While Jane Austen's heroines lived in genteel abundance, with their ample annual incomes and superfluous dishes of meat at all of their social gatherings, they also had periods of "nothingness," albeit in very gentle doses. These periods of going without were unlike our less fortunate heroines, in that they never foreshadowed starvation, but they did serve a very useful purpose for both body and soul. They fasted.

Now, Jane Austen's Anglican characters would likely have fasted for religious purposes, but we're speaking here of an extension of the kind of fasting we all do every day: that is, the pause our digestive systems receive between dinner and breakfast.

In his book, *The Jane Austen Diet*, Bryan Kozlowski makes the brilliant observation that Jane Austen and her characters were naturally fasting at least twelve hours a day: two hours after dinner, plus eight hours of sleep, plus two hours between waking up and "breaking fast" with breakfast.

Common sense would tell us that not eating when one is not hungry is a reasonable way to maintain a healthy weight, but the modern diet industry has bamboozled us into the falsehood that our bodies are something to outsmart—that they are actually not on our team!

Instead of listening to our own hunger cues, we've been persuaded to "eat six small meals a day to keep your metabolism going," "eat breakfast as soon as you put your feet on the floor," etc. It's no wonder it's so hard to listen to our bodies when the voices of others are so much louder.

The heroines spent a lot of time preparing, eating, and cleaning up food. But as we've established (and delighted over) it was never out of fear. Rather, it was out of gratitude for all the nourishing that was happening within their bodies; the strengthening up that was happening inside their bones and preparing them for all the personal growth they must undergo. Pre-diet culture, the heroines had this advantage: to hear the cues their bodies were sending them, and to trust them. They could eat, and then forget about food, leaving them more time and energy to fight the battles that would truly make them heroines.

Back to fasting: If you've ever wondered how fasting (for religious reasons or from necessity) seems to lead to vitality, the recent scientific studies on fasting in humans—when the body is not having to focus entirely on digesting food—are compelling.

In a 2019 article of the *New England Journal of Medicine,* Dr. de Cabo and Dr. Mattson write, "Evidence is accumulating that eating in a 6-hour period and fasting for 18 hours can trigger a metabolic switch from glucose-based to ketone-based energy, with increased stress resistance, increased longevity, and a decreased incidence of diseases, including cancer and obesity."

The benefits of fasting were inspired in large part by the work of Yoshinori Ohsumi, winner of the 2016 Nobel Prize in Medicine for his groundbreaking work on an incredible function of the human body called autophagy. In overly simplified terms, autophagy is our body's natural recycling program, which happens on a cellular level. Nature intended for our bodies to make use of this amazing renewal system on a regular basis, but it only goes into effect when—here's the kicker—we regularly get into a fasted state.

Gin Stephens explains autophagy in her meticulously researched book, *Fast. Feast. Repeat.* There she describes why and how autophagy is one of the most exciting benefits of intermittent fasting.

She writes, "…our bodies are designed to be metabolically flexible. Before our modern era, our ancestors had to hunt and gather to be fed, so they would have periods of time where they were naturally in the fasted state. They relied on ketosis to fuel their brains, giving them the mental clarity and energy to go out and find the food they needed. This metabolic flexibility would have gotten them through both the daily quest for food and the lean times…When autophagy is blocked somehow within the body, this can lead to the onset of cancer, liver disease, aging, metabolic syndrome, or neurodegeneration."

When we speak of intermittent fasting, we simply mean consuming only water, black coffee, or plain teas in your "fasting window" (which do not disrupt insulin levels—the key to fasting healthfully!) and eating delicious and nourishing foods according to your hunger cues, in your "feasting window." The amount of time you feast and fast is customizable to your lifestyle, but current studies support a fasting time of at least eighteen hours for optimal health benefits. So, for example, following an 18/6 protocol would mean fasting for eighteen hours (this includes the time you are sleeping!), and eating according to hunger cues in the remaining six hours.

As it so happens, Lorilee and I are big fans of this lifestyle, not only because of the countless physical benefits we continue to experience, but also because it is completely compatible with a heroine mindset: abundance can be found within limitations!

JENNY CONVINCES LORILEE TO KWIT KASUAL KETO

Lorilee and Jenny met for the first time on the Great Plains of Oklahoma, when Lorilee flew from her home in Michigan to the Williams home for a few days. The purpose was primarily to cement a previously online friendship, but also to write out the first outline of this book.

One morning, Lorilee casually mentioned to Jenny that she was doing "Kasual Keto-Casual with a K." It was so Kasual, in fact, she would gladly have a piece of the pumpkin baked oatmeal Jenny had made for her guest's breakfast. Jenny sensed a loss of freedom in this remark that compelled her to blurt out in pure sympathy, "Oh, I have something much easier than that!" And proceeded to explain the gentle lifestyle of Intermittent Fasting which she had begun a few months prior. "I drink black coffee and water when I wake up, until one o'clock, when I have a snack, and then eat salad and pizza and sometimes a glass of wine for dinner, and brownies for dessert," she said quite brazenly.

Lorilee, being the good sport that she is, declared she would give it a try and started the very next morning. She has never looked back. Both of us have experienced total food freedom in this lifestyle, along with guilt-free eating and all the benefits of autophagy and decreased inflammation! Not only do we get to eat all the foods we enjoy, but we also save time and money. (Jenny likes to call IF the eating lifestyle that seems too good to be true, but isn't.)

Honestly, there's something about the daily practice of *delaying* instead of *denying* (in the words of Gin Stephens) the foods you want that makes food taste better. When fear is removed, healing can begin. And when the science is there to support this ancestral way of eating, it's winner-winner, chicken dinner. (Eaten, of course, during one's feasting window!)

 ## HEROINE TAKEAWAYS

Now we turn our attention to some practical ways to feed ourselves and others by meal planning, utilizing leftovers, and stocking our pantries like a heroine. But first, it's over to that picnicking queen Katy Carr, who, at fourteen, learns that life is not always a picnic, nor is nourishing a family every day an easy task. For anyone who ever longed for a cooking fairy to appear in your home at about 5 p.m., read on to know you are not alone.

◉ FEEDING FATIGUE IS REAL: For many of us, we don't just have to feed ourselves, we have to feed our families, too. And sometimes, the sheer repetition of having to be the one to rustle up nourishment for a bunch of humans gets a wee bit, oh, *relentless*.

You've seen the meme: "Who knew that the hardest part of being an adult is figuring out what to cook for dinner every single night for the rest of your life?"

"Until you die," we would add.

Katy Carr, of *What Katy Did*, wasn't even a grown up and she had feeding fatigue. As the oldest daughter of a motherless household, it fell upon her to plan meals for her household, which consisted of her widowed father, herself, and a pack of younger siblings. Bedridden though she was, Katy took her role as lady of the house seriously.

"Let me see—there is roast beef—leg of mutton—boiled chicken," she would say, counting on her fingers,…"Dear!—I wish somebody would invent a new animal! Where all the things to eat are gone to, I can't imagine!"

At one point, Katy was enthused about a strange recipe, for we know not what: "This looks as if it were very delicious, Debby. I wish you'd try it; take a gallon of oysters, a pint of beef stock, sixteen soda crackers, the juice of two lemons, four cloves, a glass of white wine, a sprig of marjoram, a sprig of thyme, a sprig of bay, a sliced shallot—"

Debby, the cook, was at a loss. What on earth was a "shell-out"? Yeesh. Every night was like an episode of *Chopped* run amok, with "poor Debby" as she is referred to several times, trying to concoct some semblance of a dinner from a grab bag of ingredients. (We believe "poor Debby" was driven to drink, though we are never told this explicitly.)

Thankfully, Katy calmed herself, and soon enough the mystery basket era was over at the Carr house. Debby happily reverted to "plain roast and boiled, much to the advantage of all concerned."

All's well that ends well, we say, but what about those of us who have feeding fatigue and don't have a live-in cook? Katy was on to something, even if her execution left a little to be desired. One of the best ways to fight feeding fatigue is to plan your meals in advance.

⬤ MEAL PLAN LIKE MEG MARCH: One of the only cookbooks mentioned in the heroine novels is *The Young Housekeeper's Friend*, by Mary Hooker Cornelius, or "Mrs. Cornelius" as people called her, published in 1846 and mentioned by name in *Little Women*. It was a huge bestseller, *The Joy of Cooking* of its day, and offered the young, inexperienced housekeeper loads of friendly advice in the kitchen.

For those who were "perplexed and prematurely careworn, for want of experience or a little good instruction," Mrs. Cornelius pledged "an earnest wish to render her some effectual aid."

Meg March 100 percent needed some "effectual aid" when she married John Brook and aspired to be the quintessential homemaker (one of her goals was that John should "fare sumptuously every day," so the bar was a bit high). During her newlywed "cooking mania," Meg worked diligently through every recipe of *The Young Housekeeper's Friend,* "working out the problems with patience and care."

Meg was on to something: Working through a good cookbook such as Mrs. Cornelius's is beneficial because you can learn so much, and, as a result, your cooking gets better and better. Lorilee learned to cook well with the aid of her trusty slow cooker (her children joke that they will fill a slow cooker with flowers and place it atop her coffin), and *The Fix-It and Forget-It Cookbook* by Phyllis Good. This process changed her cooking and eating life, not to mention the eating lives of her family members. As she attempted Mrs. Good's simple yet tasty recipes, she went from merely "fixing" something to eat (boiled tortellini, chicken breasts and rice, etc) to actually cooking, relishing the process as much as the results. Soon she was serving beef stews, savory soups, and tender, moist roasts, graduating to slightly more complex cookbooks, such as *The Asian Slow Cooker* by Kelly Kwok, and anything by slow cooker goddess Stephanie O' Dea. Soon she and her family were tucking into Buttermilk Brined Whole Chicken and Korean BBQ Beef Food Truck Tacos, and it was still so easy, because, well, slow cooker. Lorilee is far too much like Anne of Green Gables—aka "dreamy," otherwise known as "featherbrained"—to stand at attention by a pan.

While Lorilee favors the slow cooker, Jenny's kitchen-hack-appliance of choice is the Instant Pot. The slow cooker is handy for the times when one knows what will be on the menu twelve hours beforehand. The Instant Pot is great for that too, but it's also there for you in the oh-no-what's-for-dinner moment around 4:00.

Jenny is the epitome of an INFP cook: a little structure with plenty of room for spontaneous creativity is the secret sauce. She enjoys meal planning, but not down to a T. There needs to be a little room for spontaneous creativity, and for that reason, the Instant Pot makes a great sous chef.

Jenny's loose formula for tasty last-minute concoctions involve a starch (rice, potatoes, pasta), fat (butter, oil, or cream), and a veggie/protein combo. On those nights, the Instant Pot is not the lead character, but rather, the lead character's upbeat and supportive best friend—she still shines! The Instant Pot is steaming broccoli or cooking rice while Jenny's tossing chicken in a pan with soy sauce, maple syrup, and cashews. With three young children, tis the season of life where dinner coming together in half an hour is a must, and the Instant Pot is here to say, "be the heroine of your dinner hour, not the victim!"

Slow cooker or pressure cook, we feel all the heroines from perfectionist Meg to forgot-to-cover-the-pudding-bowl Anne would have embraced one or the other, or both.

As it happens, both really lend themselves to meal planning, which is another heroine culinary move.

According to a 2016 consumer survey by The Hartmann Group, 53 percent of dinners are planned within an hour of eating them. Sounds stressful to us, and not at all the way our literary nourishers would have done things, because after all, there was no deli counter or ready-to-buy rotisserie chicken in Avonlea.

"I've found that taking just 30 minutes before I grocery shop sets the tone for smooth sailing in the kitchen all week," writes Carolyn Williams, Ph.D, RD, in an article for *Cooking Light* magazine. "Meal planning is what gives you ingredients and resources to actually make (eating better) happen on a daily basis."

It also saves money—like, a ton. A 2018 Forbes study found that it costs five times more to order a dish from a restaurant than it does to cook at home. Stephanie O'Dea has some fun "Fake Out Take Out" recipes on her blog, www.ayearofslowcooking.com, including Mongolian Beef, Pasta Fagioli, and Chimichangas. Meal planning also reduces food waste, because you have a plan, and if you have the ingredients in your house, you are likely to stick to it.

Katy Carr would definitely concur with Carolyn Williams's top motivation for meal planning: "Want to know what I consider the biggest perk of meal planning for my life? I don't have that nagging, late-afternoon stress associated with deciding what to do for dinner. I know that may sound silly—especially when comparing that to the health, financial, and food waste benefits—but decision fatigue is a real thing."

To sum it up, save yourself a lot of stress, time, and money by adapting a meal plan to your weekly routine. The results will surprise you, and you may even, like Meg March hoped her husband would do, "always dine on sumptuous fare," or if not sumptuous, scrumptious and nourishing.

🌀 LUSTROUS LEFTOVERS: Lorilee knew a chef once who turned up his nose at leftovers, refusing to ever cook with them! This still makes her shake her head, a decade later. Leftovers are simply everything when it comes to nourishing oneself and family on a budget.

In *The Secret Garden Cookbook* by Amy Cotler, she writes that even in the manor house, leftovers were whipped up from "the remains from the previous night's dinner."

"Lunch might include minced mutton or game pies prepared from uneaten game," Cotler says. "...All leftovers would be well garnished and disguised as another meal by the cook."

Leftovers were so well used by home cooks that there was an old English saying that explains how a large Sunday joint of meat would be served each day of the week:

Hot on Sunday
Cold on Monday
Hashed on Tuesday
Minced on Wednesday
Curried on Thursday
Broth on Friday
Cottage Pie on Saturday

For us, it would be more like:

Hot on Monday
Stir Fry on Tuesday
Soup on Wednesday
The End. Repeat.

Seriously, stir fry is a fantastic way to use up various meats (especially pork roast, a leftover powerhouse), rice, and vegetables. We've used brussels sprouts, asparagus, green beans, and corn in our leftover stir fries—no need to strictly use "stir fry vegetables" such as sugar snap peas, baby corn, water chestnuts, and red peppers.

Roasted chicken legs are a delicious, cheap, old-fashioned comfort food that practically begs to be used in a soup the next day. Just add chicken broth, garlic, leftover vegetables, and starchy odds and ends from your pantry such as that quarter-full box of lasagna noodles, broken into pieces. Mirepoix (we love Trader Joe's version of onions, carrots, and celery) is the ultimate soup starter, and when you whisk in leftover heavy cream, the result is a luxurious, sippable soup everyone will rave about.

We had to look up "Cottage Pie," which refers to a meat pie made with chopped beef, and with a "crust" made from mashed potato, rather than a traditional pastry. So basically, a Shepherd's Pie, that standby of Lorilee's Canadian childhood. A Cottage Pie (and Shepherd's Pie) was a standard way of using leftover roasted meat from the Sunday roast.

Sometimes, though, leftovers can be all wrong. We think of "cold ditto," the unappetizing name for the remains of a mutton roast, the partaking of which was seared into the minds of the Meredith children of *Rainbow Valley*, the seventh book in the *Anne of Green Gables* series. In a scene infused with the senses, the Merediths, children of the widowed minister, catch a whiff of fresh trout being grilled outdoors.

"'We had only bread and molasses for supper and cold ditto for dinner,' said Una plaintively." Of course, today one can find, with a few clicks, any number of delicious renderings of leftover mutton: lamb stew, curried lamb, roast lamb gyro with tzatziki sauce, and on and on. Perhaps Aunt Martha, their cook, was unaware of tzatziki sauce, but we think the dear lady was just sorely lacking in the imagination department.

"Aunt Martha's habit was to boil a large slab of mutton early in the week and serve it up every day, cold and greasy, as long as it lasted. To this Faith, in a moment of inspiration, had given the name of 'ditto', and by this it was invariably known at the manse."

At one point, even Aunt Martha herself admits what is in the pantry: "There's a plenty o' cold biled meat and bread and you kin try your hand at making porridge."

Cold "biled" meat!

It really sounds awful, doesn't it? It's no wonder the Meredith small fry scrabbled over the hill to find out where that tantalizing smell was coming from. And when they did come upon Anne and Gilbert's children, they were warmly welcomed into the fold and fed fresh trout, lonely no more.

- STOCK YOUR PANTRY LIKE A HEROINE: "Momma opened boxes of crispy crackers and we sat around the meat block at the rear of the Store," wrote Maya Angelou in *Caged Bird*. "I sliced onions, and Bailey opened two or even three cans of sardines and allowed their juice of oil and fishing boats to ooze down and around the sides. That was supper."

Maya Angelou's Momma ran a grocery store, so maybe it's not fair to compare her pantry to our own, but this beautiful passage bears repeating. Pantry meals are the best! Not only do you use up what's on hand, but you also save time and money. Shopping in your own pantry is like shopping in your own closet—el cheapo and so gratifying. Perhaps the term "cheap thrill" even originated from a frugal wordsmith who, instead of ordering pizza, made pizza chili in the slow cooker, utilizing usual suspects such as canned pizza sauce, pepperoni, stewed tomatoes and—the queen bee of pantry items forevermore—kidney beans. (Or black beans. Lorilee's husband, upon finding out their new Guatemalan international student was a vegan, brought home every can of black beans within a ten-mile radius.)

A well-supplied kitchen pantry will prepare you well for the likely eventuality that you will need to whip up something for dinner and you don't have time for a grocery run (or maybe you just don't feel like leaving the house).

Stocking a pantry like a heroine means you have the prime and basic ingredients for your favorite recipes on hand at all times.

In her book, *The Art of Pantry Cooking*, Ronda Carman shares how the Covid pandemic inspired her to rethink how she stocked her pantry. "During a time of not wanting to make too many trips to the supermarket, I was reminded that essential supplies are a must. Without key staples, cooking can be challenging. Having a well-stocked pantry allows you to easily create delicious and beautifully seasoned dishes."

Her list of pantry staples include familiar basics, like coconut milk, honey, lentils, olives, quinoa, and tuna, to unusual, but inspired staples like pine nuts, capers, artichoke hearts, espresso powder, and XO sauce. From baking supplies, like sugar and flour, to canned goods, spices, and condiments, staying on top of your pantry inventory will help you create so many meals in a pinch, meals that will impress yourself and those whom you are tasked to feed and nurture. Furthermore, a strategically stocked pantry is the perfect recipe for creative meals in a jiffy: we have the limitation of only using what we have, so we don't have to waste brain cells imagining what cannot be. But really, the possibilities that lie within eggs, cream, flour, coconut milk, and a few canned goods? That could keep one twirling one's hair while gazing at the Lake of Shining Waters for *hours*.

Speaking of must-have canned goods, Lorilee bestows the Golden Can Award to coconut milk, for its simplicity of use, and how it adds a lustrous creaminess to so many dishes (see "Meat Like a Heroine" in Chapter 7 for more on this magic ingredient and a recipe for venison that will really puff your sleeves, if you get our drift). It makes dishes like this one so good and so easy.

As for Jenny, her Golden Can Award goes to canned salmon. Canned salmon is incredibly versatile. Not only does it make a great quick lunch when used like canned tuna (mixed with a little mayo on bread or used as a dip for pita chips), it becomes surprisingly fancy when turned into salmon cakes, and surprisingly rich and comforting when turned into salmon chowder (made with coconut milk, no less!).

Canned salmon is the cute floral dress in your closet, for your pantry: it can be dressed up or dressed down, worn with heels and a cardigan, or with sneakers and a denim jacket. Smothered in coconut milk for a simple salmon curry, it would probably get on the best dressed list every time. If you don't already keep it in your pantry, try buying a few cans and marvel at what you can come up with next time you're tapping your chin around 4:00 p.m.

FIND THE JOY OF COOKING AGAIN

Take a minute to identify any ways you aren't enjoying food, or food preparation, at the moment. Are you in a recipe rut? Do you have picky eaters in your family who are deflating your earnest cooking efforts? Is your pantry organized in such a way that makes it difficult to find what you are looking for? Are you scrambling at 5:00 most nights, wishing a house elf would show up at your door?

Sit back, take a breath, and put food squarely back in its place: it was not created to be a burden. Food is one of life's great enjoyments, a gift to ourselves and others—a kind of love you can see! We all grow food weary at times, but thankfully, there are a myriad of remedies awaiting the cook who's running on empty.

Pour yourself a cup of tea on a Sunday afternoon and spend some time perusing your cookbook collection. If meal planning feels a little overwhelming, try planning just a few of the week's dishes instead of all of them. On the nights when you don't have a dinner planned, try omelets or stir fry or a frittata using whatever you can find in your fridge. Organize your pantry and throw out everything that is expired. Consider adding a few storage containers that are unnecessarily pretty! Start where you are, with what you have, and nourishing yourself and your loved ones will begin to feel like a gift once again.

Nourishing & Delicious Chicken Pot Pie Soup

Adapted from *The Wellness Mama Cookbook* by Katie Wells

This might look like any other chicken soup, but do not be deceived: it's surprisingly delicious! While fresh garlic is usually superior, garlic powder makes this dish sing (along with the slight sweetness of the peas and coconut milk).

Ingredients

4 Tbsp. butter

1 lb. skinless, boneless chicken breasts

4 carrots

4 celery ribs

1 onion

3 Yukon Gold potatoes, peeled

4 C of chicken bone broth

1 C coconut milk or cream*

1 tsp. salt

½ tsp. freshly ground black pepper

1 tsp. garlic powder

½ tsp. dried thyme

1 10-oz. package frozen peas

2 Tbsp. arrowroot powder

1. In a large soup pot over medium-high heat, melt the butter. Chop the chicken into ½ inch or smaller cubes and add to the pot. Cook for 5-7 minutes, until the chicken is white on all sides. Remove the chicken from the pot and set aside.

2. Chop the carrots, celery, onion, and potatoes and place in the pot. Sauté for approximately five minutes, until the vegetables start to soften. Stir in the broth and coconut milk or cream. Add the salt, pepper, garlic powder, and thyme.

3. Simmer for 10 minutes, or until all the vegetables have softened. Return the chicken to the pot and add the peas. Simmer for 2-3 more minutes, until the chicken is completely cooked through and not pink in the middle.

4. Sprinkle the arrowroot into the pot, stir, and allow the broth to thicken slightly.

5. Optional: serve with a biscuit split down the middle, right on top, if you want a more "pot pie" experience.

Coconut milk will give this soup a slight hint of sweetness that is reminiscent of chicken pot pie. If you are dairy-free, use coconut milk, and olive oil instead of butter. Cream is delicious too, although possibly too rich for a convalescing stomach.

Eating in RHYTHM WITH THE Seasons is NATURALLY ACCOMPANIED BY slowing down, NOTICING, and LIVING IN THE PRESENT ALL wonderful antidote to INFORMATION OVERLOAD AND decision-fatigue in our MODERN LIVES.

Chapter 7

EAT LOCAL LIKE A HEROINE

How Bookish Stars Thrived on Eating Rooted to Land and Seasons

"The garden is amazing—we have beets
and greens, splendid potatoes."

EMILY DICKINSON

PROBLEM: You want to eat more seasonally and wholesomely, more rooted to the land but without spending a lot of money. You want to become more intimately connected with sourcing your food and learning where it comes from. But you have no idea where to start, even if you can afford a lifestyle shift toward eating locally. Part of you wonders if eating locally is for other people, not you.

HEROINE SOLUTION: The heroines have much to teach us about how cooking with locally sourced ingredients is not only budget friendly, but healthier and more delicious. They give us ample motivation to give our food-sourcing habits a major tweak, boosting flavor, nutrients, the environment, and our local economies. A quadruple win!

"GATHER YOUR GOOSEBERRIES when ripe, top and tail!" urges Mrs. Rundell, the Betty Crocker of Jane Austen's day, in her 1806 cookbook. Our heroines embraced ripeness, whether it was Emma Woodhouse picking strawberries at Donwell Abbey, Esperanza Ortega harvesting elephant heart plums, or Laura Ingalls making Maple Sugar candy from freshly tapped trees. We do admit, they didn't exactly have a choice. It was embracing a locally sourced, seasonal diet, or nothing. The point is, the heroines flourished and bloomed as a result of their local, seasonal eating, and so can we.

In this chapter, we invite you to come closer to the miracle of food sprouting forth from the earth or perhaps grazing that same green earth for nourishment. There's even a section called "Meat Like a Heroine," inspired by Maya Angelou's description of processing farm fresh pork each year of her childhood. We may not be able to drink milk *straight up out of a goat*, like Heidi, but we can learn to eat more locally sourced, seasonal food, and we will be the better for it.

THE CREATIVE POSSIBILITIES OF BOUNDARIES

Whether our heroines simply ordered the menu (Emma Woodhouse) or were actively involved in the process of obtaining and preparing the meals that sustained them (Laura Ingalls Wilder), all of them were limited by the food they could obtain locally, and the food that was currently in season. No matter their food whims and cravings, they had to make the most of seasonal fare. Take Jane Austen herself, who set up housekeeping with her sister, mother, and close friend Martha Lloyd in a small cottage on the grounds of her brother's estate in Hampshire.

"The Austen and Lloyd women ate well," writes Reina Gattuso in an article about Austen and food. "They kept a large vegetable garden, chickens, and, sometimes, bees, and had ample access to meat and poultry from local farms and hunting grounds...Martha Lloyd's recipes reflect this rural abundance. Lloyd's recipe for 'Swiss Soup Meagre,' for example, calls for cabbage, endive, sorrel, 'Spinnage,' cherville, chives, onions, parsley, beet leaves, cucumbers, peas, and asparagus."

Karana of *Island of the Blue Dolphins* is undoubtedly our most locavore of the heroines. When she finds herself accidentally left behind on her home island for the foreseeable future, she must learn to fend for herself in every way. Talk about limitations! No general store, and no community. Not only does she eat what is available to her in the moment and within arm's reach (mostly abalones—a kind of shellfish, fish, and roots) but she eats out of locally made utensils and cookware—made by her own hands, of course. Heidi, another local queen, thrives on goat's milk that travels the short distance from stable to cottage, and feasts on the grandfather's homemade bread and cheese.

Today, these limitations aren't as relatable. We can buy berries all year round and we can find the ingredients for ethnic dishes at our local ethnic markets. The options for what we eat are seemingly endless.

The heroines's dependency on creating meals according to limited resources can help us build a deeper appreciation for the time and season we are currently in. If one could *only* eat a strawberry in the spring, how it would be relished!

Walking into a grocery store without a plan is overwhelming. But if you knew, like Ma Ingalls, that you only had a few ingredients to work with for that evening's meal, your creativity might have more room to flourish within the limitations set before you.

But aside from the creative benefits and a deeper connection to the present, there were, and remain, many health (and soul) benefits of eating like a heroine, in concert with the seasons, and with respect and support for local farmers and their land. Eating local is the best recipe we can think of for nourishing and flourishing.

 ## Heroine Takeaways

- Listen to the beating heart of the land: Local eating begins with a reverence for the land, an awe shared by many of our heroines. In *Esperanza Rising,* young Esperanza learns to love the land that grows their food and food for many others.

"Our land is alive, Esperanza," said Papa... "Did you know that when you lie down on the land you can feel it breathe? That you can feel its heart beating?"

"Papi, I want to feel it," she said.

They both lay down on the earth and listen and feel.

"She pressed closer to the ground, until her body was breathing with the earth's. And with Papa's. The three hearts beating together."

Later in the book, after Esperanza's fortunes have reversed and she has lost her cherished Papa, her love for the land continues, even as she works long hours in the hot California sun as a farmworker, sorting peaches, nectarines, and plums. "Esperanza loved the elephant heart plums. Mottled green on the outside and bloodred on the inside, they were tangy and sweet at the same time. She stood in the midsummer sun during her lunch break and ate one, bent over so the juice wouldn't run down her chin." She can taste the beating heart of the land in those vibrant plums.

Cassie Logan of *Roll of Thunder, Hear My Cry,* also has a rich heritage of love for the land. One of the most evocative and tender scenes in the book is when Cassie's papa teaches her the expansive lessons of one of their trees: "That fig tree's got roots that run deep, and it belongs in that yard as much as that oak and walnut. It keeps on blooming, bearing good fruit year after year, knowing all the time it'll never get as big as them other trees. Just keeps on growing and doing what it gotta do. It don't give up. It give up, it'll die. There's a lesson to be learned from that little tree, Cassie girl, 'cause we're like it. We keep doing what we gotta, and we don't give up. We can't."

"WE RECKON YOUR COMING BY THE FRUIT": PAY ATTENTION TO WHAT'S GROWING WHEN: Emily Dickinson grappled with agoraphobia for much of her adult life, but she found deep comfort and joy in watching the seasons change on the Dickinson property in Amherst, MA., and inspiration in the rotating menu of fresh fruits, vegetables, and even chestnuts—glorious abundance from the land. The poet would take daily walks on the homestead, delighting in what was growing and when it was ripe for the picking. "Emily enjoyed watching the produce grow and change with the seasons and was very moved by it," writes Arlyn Osborne.

Her letters and poems reveal how enthralled she was with watching food grow, from the fruits of the orchards to the vegetable plots to the chestnuts scattered on the ground on an October morning:

"Our apples are ripening fast. I am fully convinced that with your approbation, they will not only pick themselves but arrange one another in a basket and present themselves to be eaten."

"I wish you could have some cherries—if there was any way we would send you a basket of them—they are very large and delicious and are just ripening now."

"We reckon your coming by the fruit. When the grape gets by, and the pippin and the chestnut—when the days are a little short by the clock and a little long by the want—when the sky has new red gowns and a purple bonnet…"

"The beans we fricasseed and they made a savory cream in cooking." (From a letter to her cousins, which also included a dainty pressed insect within the envelope. A poet, a baker, and an armchair entomologist? Our Emily could do it all.)

In her gorgeous cookbook inspired by Emily's love for food, Osborne includes many recipes that make the most of the bountiful, seasonal produce which grew on the Dickinson homestead.

She suggests a vegetarian niçoise salad, "bursting with color and texture," crammed with all the ingredients that would have been found in Emily's garden, including potatoes, green beans, beets, and cherry tomatoes.

Sublime, and so fresh and restorative! Yes, Emily had a hard life in some ways, but the way local, seasonal food sustained and infused her body, soul, and poetry inspires and encourages us. How can we taste Emily's local eating lifestyle, even if we don't happen to live on a homestead? We are so glad you asked…

4 WAYS TO EAT LOCAL LIKE A HEROINE:

1. **Signing up for a CSA.** Community Supported Agriculture (CSA) can be one of the best ways to support local farmers in your community while also eating in season, sustainably, and very, very well. Not familiar with CSAs? Essentially, a farm gives community members a chance to purchase "shares" of their farm. In exchange for purchasing a share, you get a box of produce (usually weekly) throughout the harvest season. It's like purchasing a monthly subscription to getting fresh produce from the farm, and it's so much fun to see what appears in your basket each week—say, Rainbow Swiss Chard—and then finding recipes to go with it.

2. **Grow your own or join a community garden.** Lorilee is a houseplant maven whose husband is the gardener in the family. She relishes the end of August and the bumper crop of tomatoes

from their side-yard garden. Though she doesn't love tomato sandwiches quite as much as Harriet the Spy, she is certainly a big fan. Nothing tastes better than a fresh, vine-ripened tomato!

3. **Become a fixture at your farmer's market.** Oh, the glories of a basketful of goodies from the Farmer's Market! The food is so much fresher than what's at your grocery store; often, it has been harvested the very day you buy it, which is a far cry from most—but not all—produce to be found at the grocery store, which has probably been hauled across the country in a semi.

4. **Be attentive to what's grown locally at your grocery store.** A simple Google search reveals that currently, asparagus, leafy greens, potatoes, rhubarbs, and peas are in season in Michigan, where Lorilee lives. Meanwhile, in Oklahoma, well, it's pretty much just a variety of lettuce. But that will change next month! Pay attention to labels that indicate if the produce was grown in your state, and watch for signs that say, "locally grown." It's easy to find out what's growing in your neck of the world. The Spruce Eats and other websites offer month-by-month guides to seasonal fruit and vegetables in each state and province.

○ MEAT LIKE A HEROINE: There's *so much food* in the Little House books by Laura Ingalls Wilder, and the very first food mentioned in any of the books in that beloved series is venison, in *Little House in the Big Woods*:

"Pa had shot the deer the day before and Laura had been asleep when he brought them home at night and hung them high in the trees so the wolves could not get the meat. That day Pa and Ma and Laura and Mary had fresh venison for dinner. It was so good that Laura wished they could eat it all. But most of the meat must be salted and smoked and packed away to be eaten in the winter."

One of Lorilee's first introductions to Doyle's family was a Sunday dinner at his grandma's house. Darling, feisty little Grandma Finney served rabbit as the entrée. Little did Lorilee know this was just the beginning of many meals with fresh game as the centerpiece. Over the years, she has learned to savor venison and appreciate its many sterling qualities as a meat. When properly prepared, venison is tender and mouthwatering, with one-third the fat, cholesterol, and calories of beef.

Laura Ingalls knew it way back in the Big Woods; venison is good stuff, packed with protein, flavor, and nutritional value. Also, venison has none of beef's PR issues, including problematic sourcing from slaughterhouses that may not treat their cows well, and the environmental harm perpetuated by the beef industry.

What's a heroine to do? Eat venison like Laura, or Jane Austen, who writes in *Pride and Prejudice*, "The venison was roasted to a turn—and everybody said they never saw so fat a haunch." And if you don't have a hunter in your family or among your acquaintances, perhaps you could buy venison at the farmer's market, a goldmine of locally sourced food.

Dear reader, let's keep talking deer meat. What do you do with it once you have it? Some people don't care for the sometimes-gamey taste of venison, which depends on the animal and how it has been butchered. Lorilee's solution is to plunk that frozen slab of venison in the slow cooker and smother it in coconut milk and/or sauce (spaghetti sauce, garam masala sauce, etc.), press a button or two, and wait a few hours, luxuriating in the knowledge that a gorgeous meal is underway and she is popping bonbons on the couch. Seriously, venison doesn't taste all that different from beef when it is prepared with sauces and spices.

Teresa Lynn, from henscratches.com, advises marinating venison in buttermilk or whole milk for at least four hours. "The fat in the milk absorbs the gamey odors, and the lactic acid and calcium both act as tenderizers by breaking down the proteins and softening the collagen."

She instructs her readers to use backstrap, "the best cut of venison," cut into pieces about a centimeter thick, marinated in fatty milk, sprinkled with flour, and pan fried for a succulent entrée.

MAYA ANGELOU AND FARM-RAISED PORK SAUSAGE

Maya Angelou and Laura Ingalls Wilder, our favorite literary food writers, are probably besties in Heaven, comparing notes about how Maya rapturously recounted a secret recipe for barbeque sauce and Laura wrote thirty pages on maple syrup. In *I Know Why the Caged Bird Sings*, Dr. Angelou even captivates us with her description of processing farm pork and beef into sausages.

"The missionary ladies of the Christian Methodist Episcopal Church helped Momma prepare the pork for sausage. They squeezed their fat arms elbow deep in the ground meat, mixed it with gray, nose-opening sage, pepper and salt, and made tasty little samples for all obedient children who brought wood for the slick black stove."

(Honestly, that woman could write about anything—apparently, including sausage—and we'd be transfixed.)

In the last ninety years or so, since the days of Maya's Momma processing fresh sausage, we have gotten away from farm-to-fork practices as large supermarkets, busier lifestyles, and online stores became the norm. But the tide toward local eating is on the rise, as we understand more and more what we've been missing.

Eating meat like Laura and Maya may take some intentionality, but the benefits are manifold. Local farmers often have a deep respect for animals and raise them in ethical ways. Whether you participate in a cow/pig share or buy your meats from a farmer's market, it's a good feeling to know that, prior to starring on your dining room table, the animals you eat were living their best lives. Lorilee will never forget being handed a package of organic pork sausage by Fervid Farmer Mary, a staple at her local farmer's market.

"I knew this animal by name," FFM uttered solemnly, in tones of intensity, usually reserved for sacred oaths, or the National Security Commission. Lorilee got the message loud and clear and ate that delicious pork with a clear conscience.

● GO FRUIT PICKING, BUT DON'T BRING AUGUSTA: Dear me, shall we go strawberry picking with Emma Woodhouse or nut gleaning with Louisa Musgrove? This would be a quandary, indeed, if one lived in the Jane Austen multiverse and could travel from book to book, interacting with characters and of course, sourcing local eats with them.

Louisa Musgrove was a side character in *Persuasion*, a well-bred acquaintance of our heroine Anne Elliot, who not only famously jumped off a steep flight of stairs in Lyme—the result of her refusal to give in to, ahem, *persuasion*—but who fancied nut gleaning as a pastime. While we applaud her efforts to scour the woods of Regency England for chestnuts, walnuts, and hazelnuts, we would be too worried about her leaping from some grassy edifice on a whim to fully enjoy the outing.

Strawberry picking with Emma Woodhouse, the star of *Emma*, might work, if it were not for Augusta Elton, her picking companion. Now *that* is an annoying fictional woman. She drones on and on about strawberries as if she invented them, before getting hot and tired and turning on the fruit completely, pronouncing them "inferior to cherries."

Nonetheless, as these heroines and anti-heroines show us, it's fun and delicious to gather fruits or nuts in their season, because there is simply nothing better than eating things at the peak of freshness.

THE GROWTH THAT COMES WITH "PUTTING DOWN ROOTS"

When Jenny was ten years old, her family moved to the country. On one corner of the hundred and five acres sat a one-hundred-year-old farmhouse, and near it, a "well house" (where the laundry was done), a spooky cellar for storing canned goods and sheltering during tornado season, and a giant barn with an even spookier musty basement where the ghosts of milking cows seemed to linger.

For her parents, there were many "what have we done?" moments in the beginning. For Jenny and her three siblings this was nothing less than the Little House on the Prairie Theme Park. Not long after they moved, construction on a new house on the back of the property began, and they would eventually sell much of the acreage. But it was in this old farmhouse where they lived and grew for three years, full of anticipation of what was to come.

They learned more about snakes, mice, coyotes, raccoons, horses, chickens—and living in harmony with nature than they ever imagined they would. And by the time they were finally able to move into the new house, they were officially a country family.

(The old farmhouse and outbuildings still stand, by the way, and are being lovingly restored by a new family.)

Jenny moved away from home when she went to college and became a city dweller for the next eighteen years. But recently, in an unexpected plot twist, Jenny and her family moved to a few acres of their own, just a few minutes away from where she grew up. As the Williams family begins their own journey in country living, Jenny is remembering the seeds planted in her childhood. The days of waking up early to finish her homeschool lessons so she and her sisters could play "covered wagon" in the back of the family Suburban, where they would eventually "arrive" at the miniature log cabin their dad built for them out of old railroad ties found on the property. They would sweep the floor and put a blanket in the tiny loft, where one small child could curl up comfortably. For their meals, they gathered acorns and collected plants and dried leaves to make soup, and muddy water to make coffee in their campfire pitcher.

This elaborate imaginary play was so satisfying, although at the time, Jenny didn't know exactly what longings were being satisfied. She and her sisters were connected to the land in a tactile way, feeling the dirt under their fingernails, washing it all off before bed, and beginning again the next day. They knew that to survive the mild Oklahoma winter they'd have to collect enough acorns to last several months (acorns were quite versatile, as they could also be used for bartering). So they began their work straightaway, with great purpose, and without a moment's thought to how else their time could be spent.

They weren't just playing, they were *practicing*—preparing for the routine of the grown-up world but infusing the monotony with purpose. And isn't it funny that a bowl of leaves and inedible seeds mixed with mud was a satisfying reward for their labors?

During these years of outdoor play, the nights were filled with reading the *Little House* books, *American Girl History Mysteries*, and *Anne of Green Gables* with a book light under the covers. In all of these heroine stories, there were limitations being wrestled with, for better or for worse. But it was partly the purpose with which each challenge was tackled that was so satisfying to experience through the pages.

Eating locally, whether it's from a nearby farmer or your own backyard, is a way to reconnect to this purpose. Because the aim is more than survival, it's carving out a life in between as well, within the bounds of what is before you—what you can *see*. It's Ma, adding grated carrot to her butter to make the color more golden. It's Esperanza relishing (*noticing*) the tangy sweetness of an elephant heart plum on her lunch break, a moment of deliciousness among a season of hardship. And it's Heidi eating homemade bread and cheese with her grandfather while rekindling an estranged relationship.

A connection to the food we eat is more than just a good thing to strive for. Like imaginary play, the pursuit of eating locally, and living in rhythm with the seasons is naturally accompanied by slowing down, noticing, and living in the present—a wonderful antidote to information overload and decision-fatigue in our modern lives. Knowing this is the growth that comes with rootedness, how could we pass up this opportunity to eat like a heroine?

HEROINE CHALLENGE
GET YOUR HANDS DIRTY

What are the obstacles in your life that make eating locally feel like a challenge? If it's a financial concern, work out some numbers with a pen and calculator and you might be pleasantly surprised! Jenny buys ten pounds of ground beef from a local farm every month, because when purchased in bulk, the price per pound is cheaper than any organic/grass finished beef she could find in the grocery store.

Or if you have young children who eat constantly, is there a pricey packaged snack food that could be replaced by a more filling, nutrient-dense snack made from locally sourced fruits and vegetables (smoothies or protein-laden hummus with vegetables)? There's no need to rehaul your life when attempting to implement a more locally sourced diet. It could start with a single tomato plant on your back patio that serves as a natural motivation to seek out accompanying vegetables at the farmers market for your summer salads.

Or perhaps the easiest way to begin a feeling of rootedness to the land you live on: start a compost pile! Simply by collecting fruit

(continues on next page)

and vegetable scraps, and other organic matter, and returning them to the earth instead of adding them to the landfill, you are literally changing the soil for the better by creating more nutrient-dense earth in which future plants can thrive.

Recipe

LORILEE'S BEST & EASIEST VENISON RECIPE EVER

(Perhaps you have noticed that when Lorilee calls a recipe easy, she means that a monkey could make it, if monkeys had crockpots. The can opening may be the hardest part...)

INGREDIENTS

1 can coconut milk

1 can diced tomatoes

1 Tbsp. Curry or Garam Masala

1 hunk of frozen venison roast (or beef, if you must)

INSTRUCTIONS

1. Drop hunk of frozen meat in slow cooker.

2. Plop cans of coconut milk and diced tomatoes into the slow cooker.

3. Add curry or garam masala.

4. Press the Low button for overnight, or 8 hours.

5. Walk away, blithe in the knowledge that you and your venison dish are wondrous—dare we say, "restaurant quality"?

"I THINK there were not in all THE CITY FOUR MERRIER people than the HUNGRY LITTLE GIRLS who gave away their BREAKFASTS AND CONTENTED themselves with BREAD and MILK ON Christmas morning."

—LITTLE WOMEN

Chapter 8

HOLIDAY LIKE A HEROINE

FROM FRANCIE NOLAN'S NEW YEAR'S MILK PUNCH TO HALF-PINT'S PEPPERMINT STICK FOR CHRISTMAS

"To being together, always."

A TREE GROWS IN BROOKLYN

PROBLEM: There's so much pressure to celebrate the holidays according to overblown cultural expectations. Even if you love the holidays, you may feel the pressure and the undercurrent of material expectations. The meaning of holidays, especially Christmas, can get lost.

HEROINE SOLUTION: The heroines teach us to relish the holidays while modeling how to step back from the craziness and infuse more peace and meaning in our celebrations.

*I*N *A TREE GROWS IN BROOKLYN,* Francie Nolan celebrated New Year's Eve in high style the year she sipped milk punch with her mom and brother at home. She shows us that the heroines could keep a holiday well, no matter their circumstances. Take Katy Carr, throwing a Valentine's Day picnic soiree in her bedroom, complete with a pink-iced cake and strawberry jam and donuts. Or *Persuasion's* Anne Elliot, holding "high revel" at Christmastime as she beheld food-laden trays, "bending under the weight of...cold pies." Whether it was a sparse celebration or a decadent one, the heroines model how we can hold "high revel" on holidays, too.

CHRISTMAS: GENEROSITY AND HAPPY HOME FESTIVALS

From the groaning tables of Regency England to Independence, Kansas, and beyond, we invite you to pull up a chair with us as we tour some of the most delicious and festive holiday fetes in our favorite novels.

One thing we love about celebrating Christmas is how various foods and drinks pop up at that time of year and no other. After all, nobody consumes eggnog in July. We share our heroine's glowy feelings of anticipation and wish fulfillment as we sample Jane Austen's cold pies, Maya Angelou's upside-down pineapple cake, and the Little Women's fat, brown turkey.

Let's start our reveling in Concord, Massachusetts, circa 1860, and a cozy Yuletide scene with the March family. "Merry Christmas, little daughters!" are the first words in Chapter 2, and they come from Marmee, who has just gone out into the community to offer support to an immigrant family who has fallen on desperate times.

She has borne witness to the Hummels, newcomers from Germany, a family led by a young single mother, who can barely feed her newborn baby. Six other children tangle together to stave off the chill, for they have no fire. The oldest boy had bravely gone for help, for he knew his mother and siblings couldn't survive much longer with no food or heat.

With this scene carved on her empathetic soul, Marmee arrives home to find her daughters waiting patiently for a holiday breakfast of buckwheat cakes, English muffins, and cream. But when Marmee asks her girls if they will sacrifice their lovely, longed-for meal for the Hummels, they rise up like the heroines they are, pack up the pancakes and muffins and trudge through the snow to deliver their generous offering. Along with firewood for warmth and food for gnawing bellies, the Marches deliver a compassionate presence that carries this family in their deep distress. "Mrs. March gave the mother tea and gruel, and comforted her with promises of help, while she dressed the little baby as tenderly as if it had been her own."

What tenderness and strength undergirded this gift! It was an offering that spoke volumes of care and support. *We are here. You are not alone, even at Christmas. Especially at Christmas.*

Giving has a way of transforming the giver as much or more than the recipient, and the Little Women were renewed by their gift. "And when they went away, leaving comfort behind, I think there were not in all the city four merrier people than the hungry little girls who gave away their breakfasts and contented themselves with bread and milk on Christmas morning."

Content, and changed, the March sisters proceeded with their regularly scheduled Christmas jollities, presenting their humble wrapped bundles to their mother for her delight. Jokes, teasing, affection, and coziness ensued as Marmee opened her gifts, "in the simple loving fashion which makes these home festivals so pleasant at the time, so sweet to remember long afterward."

Just one year later, their neighbor Mr. Laurence and his grandson, Laurie, dined with them for Christmas dinner, just like the chosen family they had become. Mr. March had just returned from the Civil War, where he had served as a chaplain and had nearly died from an illness. Marmee and her girls had continued to be compassionate neighbors—leaving comfort behind with each visit—to the Hummels all year long, which deepens the beauty of their Christmas celebration. That wonderful year, "there never was such a Christmas dinner as they had that day." There was a fat, browned, stuffed and decorated turkey, melt-in-your-mouth plum pudding, and "jellies," plural, which Amy "revelled like a fly in a honey pot." They toasted each other, told stories, sang songs, and savored memories—it was a happy home festival.

The Little Women knew how to keep Christmas well. Their celebrations were rich and meaningful as they practiced generosity, hospitality, and focused on their simple but beloved family traditions. And of course, they ate delicious food, from the simple bread and butter at the first Christmas to their own mouthwatering turkey with all the trimmings, fruit jellies, and plum pudding. They teach us to be generous, even as we participate in our own "happy home festivals."

As we browsed our favorite classic novels for holiday references, we found ourselves swooning over some of the delectable menus presided over by our best-loved bookish stars. Read on for a special holiday edition of Heroine Takeaways.

 ## HEROINE TAKEAWAYS

● RELAXATION AND GOOD HOLIDAY FOOD CAN WARM THE HARDEST OF HEARTS:

The *Anne of Green Gables* series by L.M. Montgomery: Christmas in *Anne of Green Gables* is the setting for one of its most memorable scenes: When Matthew gives Anne the dress with puffed sleeves. "'I don't see how I'm going to eat breakfast,' said Anne rapturously. 'Breakfast seems so commonplace at such an exciting moment. I'd rather feast my eyes on that dress.'"

In *Anne of Windy Poplars*, plum pudding was served for the Christmas in which Green Gables hosted Anne's icy-hearted colleague, Katherine Brooke. Anne diligently pursues her mission to slowly thaw Katherine's heart through a series of homespun activities.

These activities include visiting the Green Gables cellar by candlelight (charmingly spooky!) to retrieve sweet apples, munching apples and candy by the stove during a winter storm, and going on long walks from which they "came home with appetites that taxed even the Green Gables pantry." Given what we know of Marilla's pantry-stocking abilities, we are impressed.

Katherine's visit to Green Gables marked an epoch in her life. "Life already seemed warmer. For the first time it came home to Katherine that life might be beautiful, even for her."

◉ THERE'S NO TIME LIKE CHRISTMAS TO HOLD "HIGH REVEL" AND PARTY LIKE ITS 1799 (OR, TECHNICALLY, 1817):

Persuasion, **by Jane Austen:** "On one side was a table occupied by some chattering girls, cutting up silk and gold paper; and on the other were trestles and trays, bending under the weight of brawn and cold pies, where riotous boys were holding high revel; the whole completed by a roaring Christmas fire."

◉ NOTHING SAYS BONDING LIKE A CHRISTMAS FEAST WITH ALL THE FAMILY FAVORITES, PREPARED BY LOVING HANDS:

Roll of Thunder, Hear My Cry **by Mildred Taylor:** "By dawn, the house smelled of Sunday; chicken frying, bacon sizzling, and smoke sausages baking. By evening, it reeked of Christmas. In the kitchen sweet potato pies, egg custard pies, and rich butter pound cakes cooled…orange yellow yams; and a choice sugar-cured ham brought from the smokehouse awaited its turn in the oven."

◉ SOME THINGS ARE WORTH THE WAIT, LIKE MOMMA'S ONCE-A-YEAR PINEAPPLE UPSIDE DOWN CAKE!:

I Know Why the Caged Bird Sings, **Maya Angelou:** "My obsession with pineapples nearly drove me mad. I dreamt of the days when I would be grown and able to buy a whole carton for myself alone. Although the syrupy golden rings sat in their exotic cans on our shelves year-round, we only tasted them during Christmas. Momma used the juice to make almost-black fruit cakes. Then she lined heavy soot-encrusted iron skillets with pineapple rings for rich upside-down cakes. Bailey and I received one slice each, and I carried mine around for hours, shredding off the fruit until nothing was left except the perfume on my fingers."

◉ SOMETIMES THE BEST GIFTS ARE THE SIMPLEST. LAURA AND MARY TEACH US THAT WE NEED NOT BE EXCESSIVE IN OUR HOLIDAY EATING TO SAVOR THE TREATS THAT FEED OUR SOULS:

Little House on the Prairie, **Laura Ingalls Wilder:** "Then they plunged their hands into the stockings again. And they pulled out two long, long, sticks of candy. It was peppermint candy, striped red and white. They looked and looked at the beautiful candy, and Laura licked her stick, just one lick."

◉ CURRANTS, AGAIN! BUT WE DIGRESS. ACTUAL TAKEAWAY: PREPARING A HOUSE AND FOOD WITH GREAT LOVE CAN BE ONE OF THE MOST JOYFUL EXPERIENCES OF THE SEASON—ESPECIALLY IF UNDERTAKEN WITH AN ATTITUDE LIKE JANE'S:

Jane Eyre, **Charlotte Brontë:** Jane, who had been a hungry and neglected orphan for most of her life, comes into a surprise fortune right before Christmas. Anticipating a holiday visit from her cousins Diana and Mary, two of the only people who had ever been kind to her, a gleeful Jane, resourced for the first time in her life, plunges into happy and vigorous preparations to make their homecoming one they would never forget.

"My first aim will be...to clean down Moor House from chamber to cellar; my next to rub it up with beeswax, oil, and an indefinite number of cloths, till it glitters again; my third, to arrange every chair, table, bed, carpet, with mathematical precision, afterwards I shall go near to ruin you in coals and peat to keep up good fires in every room; and lastly, the two days preceding that on which your sisters are expected will be devoted by Hannah [the housekeeper] and me to such a beating of eggs, sorting of currants, grating of spices, compounding of Christmas cakes, chopping up of materials for mince pies, and solemnizing of other culinary rites..."

⬤ HANUKKAH AND CHRISTMAS ARE A "TIME OF GLADSOMENESS," ENJOYING EACH OTHER AND THE MEANINGFUL TRADITIONS AND FOODS OF THE SEASON:

The *All-of-a-Kind Family* series by Sydney Taylor: It's December circa 1912 in New York's lower East Side. Five sisters are in the kitchen of the family's four-bedroom flat, eager to help with food preparations. This "was the time for gladsomeness. It was the first night of Hanukkah—Festival of Lights—the happy holiday right in the midst of December's bleakness," Sydney Taylor writes in *More All-of-a-Kind Family*, the second book in the beloved children's series published in the 1950s.

The series follows a Jewish immigrant family with five daughters (and later a son) through eventful happenings centering around family life. This is how the entire series feels: like a warm hearth in the middle of winter.

The sisters take turns grating the ingredients for latkes, potatoes and onions, and Mama mixes them in a bowl with eggs, matzo flour, salt, and pepper.

"By this time the oil in the frying pan was bubbling hot. It sizzled a welcome to the spoonfuls of pancake mix Mama fed it. Soon a delicious aroma spread through the room. The children hung over the stove, eager for a taste of the very first hot potato pancake that would come off the fire. My, it was good! All crispy, crunchy outside, all tasty, chewy on the inside! It disappeared too quickly in the mouth, rushed down to the tummy, leaving them with a craving for more," writes Taylor.

Later, the family bundles up to walk through the snow to a Hanukkah party at Aunt Rivka's house where she serves "high mounds of steaming latkes, fruit, nuts, raisins, and dates, and finally her great specialty, rich, brown, moist slices of honey cake. Hot tea was poured into glasses for everyone."

Shortly after, Uncle Solomon brings out a dreidel, and by the end of the chapter, the reader is just as content as the young partygoers, and also craving latkes and honey cake.

> ◉ NO MATTER OUR CIRCUMSTANCES, HOPE AND TOGETHERNESS GIVE US STRENGTH, EVEN IN THE WORST OF TIMES:

A Tree Grows in Brooklyn by Betty Smith: If you read the *All-of-a-Kind Family* series growing up and then *A Tree Grows in Brooklyn*, you might delight in the very real fictional possibility that Ella, Henny, Sarah, Charlotte, Gertie, and Charlie could have walked right past Francie and Neeley Nolan given the overlapping time period and New York setting.

By the time New Year's Eve rolls around in *A Tree Grows in Brooklyn*, we are so deeply entrenched in the setting that Betty Smith has painted for us, Katie mixing up glasses of milk punch (each with a small "jiggerful" of brandy) for her children leaves us unruffled. Katie serves them spiked punch for two reasons. One, they are Irish, and two, it is a test (which she doesn't announce, of course). She watches them take what she presumes to be their first sips of alcohol and waits for any possible foreshadowing of her late-husband's fate on their faces.

"'What do we drink to?', asked Francie.

'To a hope,' said Katie. 'A hope that our family will always be together the way it is tonight…'

'To being together, always,'" says Francie.

Later when the children are alone on the roof, Francie says to her brother, "'Mama tested us when she gave us that milk punch. I know it.'

'Poor mama,' said Neeley. 'But she doesn't have to worry about me. I'll never get drunk again because I don't like to throw up.'

'And she doesn't have to worry about me, either. I don't need to drink to get drunk. I can get drunk on things like the tulip—and this night.'"

⬤ WHETHER YOU ADORE VALENTINE'S DAY OR LOATHE IT, MAYBE THIS YEAR YOU CAN MAKE IT A LITTLE MORE SPECIAL FOR WHOM-EVER YOU LOVE, BE IT A SPOUSE, LOVE INTEREST, GIRLFRIENDS, FAMILY MEMBERS, OR EVEN PETS:

What Katy Did by **Susan Coolidge:** In the post-Christmas dol-drums, bedridden Katy and her friend Cece spark up with plans for the next holiday on the horizon.

"Oh, Cecy, let's do something funny on Valentine's-Day! Such a good idea has just popped into my mind," said Katy.

A few days later, Katy's siblings came home from school and were greeted with the news that they were to wash up and make their way to Katy's bedroom for tea with Cece.

Even though Cece's presence was a daily occurrence, something was obviously afoot when they were handed "a neat little note for each, requesting the pleasure of their company at 'Queen Katharine's Palace,' that afternoon, at six o'clock. This put quite a different aspect on the affair."

When they entered Katy's room, the Carr kids beheld an irresist-ible red and pink tableau around the fireplace. "…There was a round table all set out with a white cloth and mugs of milk and biscuit, and strawberry-jam and doughnuts. In the middle was a loaf of frosted cake. There was something on the icing which looked like pink letters, and Clover, leaning forward, read aloud, 'St. Valentine.'"

After the last sugary letter was eaten, there were more surprises for the siblings: Katy had written each one a personalized poem, which were hand-delivered to them via Bridget, the maid. Clover was "perfectly enchanted," and Elsie thought it was "just like a fairy story." Dorry, Philly, and Johnny all received their valentines in turn, with the latter concluding that the whole sweet shebang had been a "funny evening."

We think by "funny" Johnny meant "singular, memorable, and festive." What could have been just another dull, wintry day was crafted by a heroine into something none of them would ever forget.

In the Time of the Butterflies by Julia Alvarez: In this modern classic, Alvarez relates a fictional account of the real-life martyred Mirabal sisters, our valorous heroines who led the underground revolution against the dictator Trujillo of the Dominican Republic. The book is written in the first and third person, by and about the Mirabal sisters, including little sister María Teresa's inspired Valentine's Day menu. "Dinner is all in my hands," María Teresa gushes in her diary.

The occasion: María Teresa's sister, Minerva (one of the gutsiest heroines ever) is bringing her "special someone," Manolo, over for dinner with the family.

"Bear in mind today is the Day of Lovers and so red is my theme," María Teresa adds before writing out her *rojo y rosa intenso* bill of fare:

Salad of tomatoes and pimientos with hibiscus garnish
Pollo a la criolla (lots of tomato paste in my San Valentin version)
Moors and Christians rice—heavy on the beans for the red brown color
Carrot—I'm going to shape the rings into little hearts
Arroz con Leche

The salad, deeply red, is self-explanatory, but we had fun looking up the juicy little details of Mate's menu. *Pollo a la criolla* is a Dominican stew with chicken, red peppers, orange juice, tomato paste, and one cup of Dominican Presidente beer. Moors and Christians is a rice dish which *Epicurious* writer Maricel Presilla called "felicitous." "For seven centuries, Moors and Christians fought one another in Spain, but in the guise of black beans and rice they surrendered to each other's charms within the all-embracing New World pot."

This festive meal was topped with dessert (because what is Valentine's Day without dessert?): Creamy, cinnamony *arroz con leche* rice pudding. No wonder the impressively dimpled Manolo "ate seconds and thirds."

Also, no wonder? María Teresa, who invested heart and soul into creating the perfect romantic menu for her sister's boyfriend, would end up marrying her own love on a future February 14. Now that's what we call a dedicated fan of Valentine's Day!

● WE CAN REMIND OUR NEAREST AND DEAREST THAT WE ARE THERE FOR THEM, AND THAT SPRING IS COMING:

Betsy-Tacy **by Maud Hart Lovelace:** "Friendship almost seems too simplistic a concept in Maud Hart Lovelace's books: these are dedicated, lifelong relationships," writes *Betsy-Tacy* admirer Marcie McCauley in an article on Literaryladiesguide.com.

Betsy and Tacy's tight bond reveals itself in the first book, *Betsy-Tacy*, when they celebrate Easter together for the first time. Under the supervision of their older sisters, the girls take a crack at dyeing Easter eggs.

"The eggs were placed in the cups for a while, and when they were taken out they were red or purple or orange. The colors were so bright... it was thrilling to look at them."

This seemingly mundane tradition turned out to be crucial in comforting Tacy when her baby sister, Bee, died soon after she and Betsy decorated the eggs.

Even in the deepest loss, the comfort of a good friend can go a long way. When the little girls are reunited after the dark days and nights following Bee's death, they take an early morning walk together in the springtime. Tacy finds a purple egg from their dyeing session in her pocket, and wonders if the birds —specifically the first robin of spring—would take the egg up to Bee in Heaven. Betsy is sure that she can and scrambles up a tall tree to place Tacy's egg in the robin's nest for its celestial delivery.

This chapter in Betsy-Tacy is very sad but ends with redemption and hope. Just as the Easter story itself features death and resurrection, this simple yet wise children's story shows a terrible loss and then the buds of new life and creativity. "It happened on the first, good, play-out Saturday in spring. The sun was warm over the earth. Robins and bluebirds and orioles flew in and out of the newly leaved maples, singing as they went."

MARK THE HOLIDAY WITH YOUR OWN PATRIOTIC TRADITIONS, SUCH AS SHEET CAKE WITH WHITE ICING AND RASPBERRIES ARRANGED LIKE THE MAPLE LEAF:

Rilla of Ingleside by L.M. Montgomery: Anne of Green Gables, meanwhile, would have celebrated Dominion Day, or what became Canada Day on July 1, when Canada was created in 1867, a confederation of colonies within British North America. The Creation of Canada Day gave loyalist Canadians the chance to whoop it up on an annual basis, just as their American neighbors had done for a century on July 4. One year after confederation, Governor General Lord Monck signed a proclamation that requested all of Her Majesty Queen Victoria's subjects across Canada to celebrate July 1.

Maud was passionately patriotic to Canada. *Rilla of Ingleside*, the eighth and final book in the Anne series, is replete with references to Canada's participation in World War 1.

In "How I Became a Writer," Maud wrote: "In my latest story, 'Rilla of Ingleside', I have tried, as far as in me lies, to depict the fine and splendid way in which the girls of Canada reacted to the Great War—their bravery, patience and self-sacrifice. The book is theirs in a sense in which none of my other books have been: for my other books were written for anyone who might like to read them: but "Rilla" was written for the girls of the great young land I love, whose destiny it will be their duty and privilege to shape and share."

● MARK THE HOLIDAY WITH YOUR OWN FLAG-WAVING TRADITION, SUCH AS EMILY DICKINSON'S FEDERAL CAKE:

The poetry of Emily Dickinson: In at least one poem, "My Country's Wardrobe," Emily Dickinson showed some serious flag waving zeal in depicting her homeland as a female who was armed and dangerous.

She also displayed her love for her country through food. According to Arlyn Osborne, Emily sent a package of patriotic Federal Cake to a friend in 1880. "Colonial Americans were faithful to England and followed their cookbooks," writes Osborne. "This eventually changed as Americans identified the need to establish their own style of cooking. Cookbooks featuring American ingredients first appeared around 1800. Foods like Federal Cake, Election Cake, and Independence Cake were a way to insert patriotism to the newly formed American Cuisine."

● NOT ONLY IS A POTLUCK MEAL THE EASIEST WAY TO GET A LARGE CROWD TOGETHER, IT'S A WONDERFUL OPPORTUNITY FOR EVERYONE TO SHARE THE FOODS THAT ARE MEANINGFUL TO THEM:

Little Town on the Prairie **by Laura Ingalls Wilder:** In *Little Town on the Prairie,* the seventh book in the Little House series, the Ingalls family is living in the town of De Smet, South Dakota for the winter. As Thanksgiving approaches, their fellow church members decide to use the day as an opportunity to raise money to pay for their church building. They decide on a New England Supper—perhaps known better to us as a "potluck"—and preparations begin with great excitement.

There was no school on Thanksgiving Day, nor any dinner. "It was a queer, blank day, full of anxious watching of the pie and the beans and of waiting for the evening." But when evening did arrive, and the Ingalls family arrives at the church, oh the feast that awaited them!

"In all their lives, Laura and Carrie had never seen so much food. Those tables were loaded," Laura writes. "There were heaped dishes of mashed potatoes and of mashed turnips, and of mashed yellow squash, all dribbling melted butter down their sides from little hollows in their peaks. There were large bowls of dried corn, soaked soft again and cooked with cream. There were plates piled high with golden squares of corn bread and slices of white bread and of brown, nutty-tasting graham bread. There were cucumber pickles and beet pickles and green tomato pickles, and glass bowls on tall glass stems were full of red tomato preserves and wild-chokecherry jelly. On each table was a long, wide, deep pan of chicken pie, with steam rising through the slits in its flaky crust.

Most marvelous of all was the pig. It stood so lifelike, propped up by short sticks, above a great pan filled with baked apples. It smelled so good. Better than any smell of any other food was that rich, oily, brown smell of roasted pork, that Laura had not smelled for so long."

The evening was a great success, on all accounts, and "It was a compliment to Ma's cooking that not a bite of the pumpkin pie nor a spoonful of the beans remained."

If getting your friends together for a specific occasion, or for no reason at all, sounds fun but impossible, a potluck might be your answer.

HEROINE CHALLENGE
BE THE HEROINE OF THE HOLIDAYS

Be the heroine of the holidays, not the victim! Even the most love-filled holidays can have their moments of anxiety. Is there a particular stressful situation or expectation you dread every year that interferes with joyful celebration? If so, if it is not something you can eliminate without an uproar from your family, can you modify it without changing it altogether, pace yourself differently, or infuse it with your own flavor? If the dreaded situation or expectation truly is outside of your control, say along with Elinor Dashwood in *Sense and Sensibility*, "I *will* be calm; I *will* be mistress of myself." And if you are able, step away, and settle in comfortably where you have complete domain, the inner sanctuary of your thoughts, where a sympathetic sister awaits you between the pages of any number of beloved heroine novels.

Recipe

LOUISA MAY ALCOTT'S APPLE SLUMP

This melt-in-your-mouth treat is perfect when served with ice cream for a Fourth of July picnic, or with bourbon (neat) at Christmas.

APPLE BASE

5 to 6 tart apples; pared, cored, and sliced (Granny Smiths work well)

Juice of ½ lemon

½ tsp. vanilla extract (or bourbon)

½ C firmly packed light brown sugar

½ tsp. nutmeg

½ tsp. cinnamon

¼ tsp. salt

TOPPING

1½ C flour

⅓ C sugar

2 tsp. baking powder

½ tsp. salt

1 egg, beaten

½ C milk

6 Tbsp. butter, melted

½ C chopped walnuts

1. Preheat oven to 350 degrees F (177 C). Grease the inside of a 9 x 13 baking dish.

2. Make apple base: In a large bowl, gently mix apple slices, lemon juice, and vanilla (or bourbon). In a small bowl, mix brown sugar, nutmeg, cinnamon, and salt. Add the sugar mixture to the apple mixture and toss until coated.

3. Spread apple base evenly in prepared pan and bake until soft, about 20 minutes.

4. Make topping: While the apples are baking, sift together flour, sugar, baking powder, and salt. Add egg, milk, and melted butter. Stir gently.

HEROINE *food fads*

TOMBSTONE SLAB
sugar cookies

AMY MARCH'S
PICKLED LIMES

CHESTNUTS

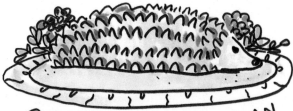

REGENCY ERA MARZIPAN
hedgehog

EMILY WEBSTER'S
shrimp wiggle

RED CURRANTS

Chapter 9

OBSESS LiKE A HEROiNE

FOOD FADS AND ODDITIES FROM AMY MARCH'S PICKLED LIMES TO JANE AUSTEN'S KILLER CYANIDE BISCUITS

"Every storm runs out of rain."

MAYA ANGELOU

(Our paraphrase: "Every trend runs out of steam.")

PROBLEM: Google knows this: We are curious little cats. We have always wondered whether Amy March's pickled limes were for actual consumption or merely used as schoolroom currency. We've heard rumors that Jane Austen's heroines served small doses of cyanide to their guests, yet none of Jane's novels are murder mysteries. We wonder, what's up with blancmange? Pies made of suet? And for the love, why does every heroine seem to yammer on about currants?

HEROINE SOLUTION: When we explore the curiosities of food in our beloved novels, we link arms with the heroines as they lead us to fascinating stories about human history, science, art, and tradition. In our modern world, food trends still abound, and in this chapter, we learn why embracing a few culinary curiosities, past or present, can add just the right amount of playfulness to your dinner party. What better way to get the conversation flowing than by asking, "Does anyone have a recipe for biscuits with trace amounts of poison?"

EARLY IN THEIR FRIENDSHIP, Jo March visits Laurie while he's suffering from a cold and brings him some blancmange. Translated in English to "white eating," blancmange is a jiggly pale pudding that was totally a thing. (Martha Stewart calls it "a large-format panna cotta," and we defer to her.) Our heroines gobbled it down hither and thither like it was going out of style, which, currently, it kind of has.

Hanging out in heroine kitchens made us realize that food is as faddish as clothing and home decor. Entrees, spices, flavorings, and cooking methods that were popular on the tables of Avonlea (1908), *Little Women's* Concord (1865), or Jane Austen's Pemberly (1808), vary widely from each other, not to mention us space-agers in the 2020s.

When was the last time you spotted blancmange at a potluck, tucked into a mince pie with suet, or had anything at all with currants in it?

According to Jenne Bergstrom and Miko Asada, authors of *The Little Women Cookbook,* not only did home cooks boil their vegetables for a mushy forty-five minutes, but there were many differences between how the March sisters would have whipped up their meals and the way we do it.

"Victorian bakers were reaching for their nutmeg where we would add vanilla, and nutmeg was also as common in savory dishes as pepper," they write. "We struggled to find a cookie recipe from the period, but there were endless options for blanc-manges and puddings."

Blancmange is just one heroine food fad that makes us go, *Hmmmm, weird*, but there are plenty more. Take the Pickled Lime Craze of the Late 1860s.

In Chapter 7 of *Little Women*, Amy's Valley of Humiliation, the youngest March girl discusses what Bergstrom and Asada call "the most iconic food item" in the book, with her sisters. "It's nothing but limes now, for everyone is sucking them in their desks in schooltime, and trading them off for pencils, bead rings, paper dolls, or something else, at recess. If one girl likes another, she gives her a lime. If she's mad with her, she eats one before her face, and doesn't offer even a suck."

Amy buys twenty-five of the "fashionable pickle," for one penny each, and, having craved them badly, eats one on her way to school. Mean girl Jenny Snow busts her, though, as pickled limes are a "contraband article" at school, and Amy ends up having to chuck all the limes out the window and be struck on the hand by one of the worst teachers in all of the heroine novels, the inept and cruel Mr. Davis.

Pickled limes weren't sweet, but rather "very bitter and rather salty—similar to the preserved citrus pickles that are still common in Middle Eastern, Indian, and Southeast Asian cooking today," write Bergstrom and Asada. They suggest that the appeal of pickled limes being traded among schoolgirls as a type of "super intense snack food," á la Flamin' Hot Cheetos and the like. Their recipe in the cookbook replicates the bitter limes that had soaked in brine for five months, the average length of time for a ship to travel from the West Indies to the East Coast of the U.S., and calls for just three ingredients: salt, water, and limes.

FLOWERY FLAVORS & JANE'S SPONGE CAKE

"Orange-flower water can give even a simple fruit salad a faraway lilt," so says *Bon Appetit*, "but adding too much of it leaves a dish tasting like old-fashioned soap."

We wonder, since rout cakes, served to Mrs. Elton in *Emma,* are laced with orange flower water, why that sourpuss didn't complain that her teatime fare tasted like soap, but Angsty Augusta would have been well used to the floral taste. We daresay—floral flavors abounded in Jane Austen's world. One recipe we found for rout cakes in *Tea with Jane Austen,* calls for flour, butter, sugar, currants (again), an egg, 1 tsp. orange flower water, and 1 tsp. rosewater. Sponge cake, lemon cheesecakes, butter buns—and that Regency favorite—the glam-yet-creepy marzipan hedgehog, all call for orange flower water or rosewater.

We are also endlessly fascinated by the fact that the first recorded use of the word "sponge-cake" is by Jane Austen, as verified in the *Oxford English Dictionary.* Besides sponge cake, Jane and her heroines were besotted with parboiled tongue, mince pies featuring suet (the raw, hard fat of beef, lamb, or mutton found around the loins and kidneys of a calf), and biscuits laced with bitter almonds, now outlawed for containing cyanide. Yes, cyanide, as in a favorite murderous poison used in Agatha Christie's novels; it causes everything from headaches to nausea to convulsions, coma, and death!

Martha Lloyd, Jane's housemate, even suggested making ratafia cakes with apricot kernels or bitter almonds. These ingredients "contain small amounts of cyanide," writes Vogler. "Bitter almonds are banned, but apricot kernels are still available." But hey, what's a little toxic crumpet between friends?

Marzipan Hedgehogs: The Showstopper Dessert of 1808

Today, unicorn croquembouche cake, cupcakes frosted with sage green icing succulents, and gin and tonic trifles are on trend as showstopping desserts for special events.

Roll back time a couple of centuries, though, and the chicest dessert you could have served at an adult party in 1808 was the marzipan hedgehog. Jane Austen and her heroines would have frequently encountered this jaunty sugar beastie, crafted from ground almonds, icing sugar, butter, and a little orange flower water "to keep them from oiling," said Hannah Glasse, author of a 1747 cookbook.

Glasse suggests stirring the mixture over a "slow fire" until stiff enough to shape into the "Form of a Hedge-Hog." Raw almonds for spikes and currants for eyeballs complete the look of the hedgie, who then wallows in a quagmire of Hartshorn jelly. (According to *Cooking with Jane Austen* by Kirstin Olsen, two types of natural gelatin used in Jane's day were "Hartshorn [from the horn of a buck] and Isinglass—a pure gelatin prepared from the air bladder of the sturgeon and certain other fishes.") All we can say is, we are glad to live in a day and age where we don't have to shave anyone's horns or procure their air bladders to make our bakes. Even unicorn croquembouche cake looks easy in comparison.

BOOZY PIES OF MEAT AND FRUIT

While dwelling on the foods and folkways of Regency and Victorian England, we can't skip that oldie deep dish, the mince pie. This pie was a favorite receptacle for meat scraps such as mutton, beef, or tongue. "If you chuse Meat in your Pies, parboil a Neat's Tongue, peel it and chop the Meat as fine as possible, and mix it with the rest," writes Hannah Glasse. Interestingly, the beef tongue would have been chopped up in the piecrust, not the filling.

Meat pies as a main dish have fallen out of fashion, with the exception of the chicken pot pie and shepherd's pie. But savory pies were a mainstay of Regency and Victorian tables. "Before the days of dietary domination by potatoes, pasta, and rice, it is not surprising that menus featured many hefty pies and tarts," writes Vogel. "Every cookbook offered a huge range of recipes for pastry or 'paste.'"

Hannah Glasse's recipe for Mince Pie called for three pounds of suet, raisins, currants, "half a hundred" pippins (apples), sugar, spices, and tons of booze: half a pint of brandy, half a pint of "Sach," or Sack, a white fortified wine imported from mainland Spain or the Canary Islands, and three spoonfuls of red wine to top it all off. "It will keep good for four months," she promises, which strikes us as true considering the pie was basically embalmed in ethanol.

Besides the meat, mince pie was essentially a fruitcake, another fad food of days gone by. Pies, both sweet and savory, were incredibly popular during Emily Dickinson's time.

In her early fifties, Emily Dickinson sent her friend Nellie her recipe for Black Cake, which has survived today and calls for two pounds of flour, five pounds of raisins, and nineteen eggs! Half a cup of molasses gives the dense fruitcake its "black" color.

"Victorian America was dazzled by color," writes Arlyn Osborne. "Black cake, silver cake, and golden cake were among the era's vibrant bouquet of desserts."

According to Jessie Sheehan, the author of *The Vintage Baker*, "Silver Cake" is actually white cake, "made with nary an egg yolk but with copious amounts of stiffly peaked egg whites. I encountered many recipes for this cake, often with slight variations on the name—Silver Sea Foam Loaf, Penny-Wise Silver Cake, and Silver White Cake."

 ## CRAZY FOR CURRANTS

We've hinted at our heroines's obsession for currants for many-a-chapter. They are sprinkled in seemingly every heroine text we pick up, and yet, who among us has ever popped one of these taut beads of juiciness into our mouths, much less baked a dozen currant buns or made red currant wine?

In *Emma*, a member of the strawberry picking party declares that currants are "more refreshing" than strawberries. Marilla's red currant wine is what Diana mistakes for raspberry cordial in *Anne of Green Gables*. It is, ironically, also the calming beverage Anne retrieves for Marilla after the passing of a harrowing storm in *Anne of Avonlea*. In *Anne of Windy Poplars*, little Elizabeth exclaims, "Red currants are such beautiful things, aren't they, Dora? It's just like eating jewels, isn't it?" In *Anne of Ingleside*, Anne invites Diana over for actual red currant wine. (No pretenses of cordial here. "Just to make us feel real devilish," she says.)

In *Jane Eyre*, Jane includes "sorting of currants" in her list of "culinary rites" in her Christmas baking preparations. *The Secret Garden*'s kind and nurturing Mrs. Sowerby is determined to help Mary and her friends get the nourishment their growing bodies need by sending them a pail of good new milk and some currant buns. And Sara Crewe, in her most princess-ly moment of largesse, shares most of her "large, plump, shiny buns, with currants in them" with a small soul even more unfortunate than herself.

(Interestingly, also in *A Little Princess*, red currant wine is among the basket of treats that Ermengarde's aunt sends her. Either Ermengarde's aunt doesn't know Ermengarde well enough to know that she is still a child, or Ermengarde knew what Diana did not: that, given its 6 percent alcohol content, it should only be wafted by children, and not consumed. Regardless, we are confused.)

There's more, but need we go on?

Currants can even be found masquerading as other fruits entirely. In recipes for plum pudding, for example, not a single plum is included in the list of ingredients, but they do call for ¾ cups of...currants!

According to the USDA Nutrition Handbook, black currants are listed as containing more vitamin C than any other available fruit, as much potassium as bananas, twice as much calcium as any fruit except blackberries, and second only to elderberries in iron and protein. As if that isn't enough, they also contain bioflavonoids, which means they contain antiviral, anti-allergy, and anti-inflammatory properties.

Currants, you cheeky little berries, what should twenty-first century heroines make of your alluring yet elusive nature? Also—we know you aren't really plums. *So where have you really gone?*

SOLVED: THE MYSTERY OF THE DISAPPEARING CURRANTS

It turns out that currants might not be included in our chapter of obsessions if it weren't for a 1920s federal law in the U.S. banning red and black currants. Not only was no one allowed to grow or import these bejeweled shrubs any longer, but there were great efforts taken during the Great Depression to eradicate the plants in the U.S. altogether. Were strawberries jealous of their "more refreshing" rivalry, you may ask? Were oranges threatened by their higher vitamin C content?

Surprisingly, it was the pine tree that was most alarmed by the unassuming three-foot bush. Somewhere around 1925, currants were found to be the unfortunate host of white pine blister rust, a fungal disease that happens to be the enemy of all five-needle pines. The prosperous timber industry was threatened, and so drastic measures were taken.

On the other hand, while currant plants were dwindling in the United States, their cultivation was encouraged in England during WWII, probably because of their high vitamin C content, and their suitability to the weather in the United Kingdom.

Eventually, in the 1960s, the U.S. government decided to leave the reversal of this ban up to individual states, and today, currants are legal again in all but five states. (They are legal in Lorilee's state of Michigan, but she would have to obtain a permit to grow them!)

This forty-year cultivation hiatus explains why we citizens of the U.S. view currants as a novelty. Now we know they didn't exactly "fade from fashion," and that today in other parts of the world, like England, you might pick up a black currant flavored popsicle or soda (Ribena) without thinking anything of it! If you do live in the U.S., however, look for them at farmers markets or ask a local farmer about them. Or better yet, see if you can plant some in your own backyard. Since the early 2000s they have started to make a comeback in some areas of the country, and wouldn't it be nice to play a small part in making them commonplace again? Perhaps one day in the not-so-distant future, you too could count sorting currants among your Christmas culinary rites.

HEROINE TAKEAWAYS

- HAVE FUN WITH ALL THE FOOD ODDITIES: One of our favorite things about Lucy Maud Montgomery was her delicious eye for the absurd. She knew how to set up a rib-tickling, ridiculous yarn to make her reader mirthfully spit out their tea. In the context of food and oddities, we love this particular little "slab" of a story:

In *Anne of Windy Poplars*, Anne is escorted by Miss Valentine Courtaloe in an informational mosey around the town cemetery; she spills the tea on any number of Summerside's dearly departed. Uncle Samuel McTabb, for example, was never really drowned at sea as it had been supposed for fifty years. When he turned up quite alive, his family took down his tombstone (as one does). When they tried to *return it* (like a pair of jeans!), the tombstone guy turned them down (as one does). Well, Mrs. Samuel wasn't going to let a little thing like her husband coming back from the dead to prevent her from using it up, wearing it out, making do, or doing without. She pronounced that old tombstone "just fine," and used it as a slab on which to roll out her dough. "The McTabb children were always bringing cookies to school with raised letters and figures on them . . . scraps of the epitaph," said Miss Valentine. "They gave them away real generous, but I could never bring myself to eat one."

We have so many questions . . .

"Save the tastefully flour dusted marble for pretty photos," urges a foodie article we found, raving about silicone baking mats. Sure, that was fine before we knew about tastefully flour-dusted tombstones.

We can just imagine those McTabb kids, generously passing out cookies to their friends, cookies that if placed together, just might read "Here lies the body of Samuel McTabb." It's true what they say: Some kids really do get the best stuff in their lunches.

● EVERYTHING OLD IS NEW AGAIN: CHESTNUTS (NOT NECESSARILY) ROASTING ON AN OPEN FIRE: Quick—what do you think of when you hear the word "chestnuts"? If it's something about roasting on an open fire, you're not alone. But our heroines devoured them.

"Chestnuts were a popular flavor choice for early American stuffing," writes Arlyn Osborne, author of *The Emily Dickinson Cookbook*. Popular, and free. "In the nineteenth century, the chestnut was a complimentary food item. New England housed millions of chestnut trees that sprinkled to the ground below with a blanket of sweet and savory nuts."

While the chestnut is not as vogue as it used to be, vegans still make good use of it. The BBC Good Food website lists a cornucopia of recipes, including mushroom and chestnut rotolo and squash steaks with chestnut and cavolo nero pilaf.

It just goes to show, sometimes our heroines were so far behind they were ahead. Next time you see chestnuts carpeting the ground on some glorious autumn day, you might think "free food" and fill your hoodie pockets with enough old-fashioned nuts to make some kind of new-fashioned dish.

● IF YOU DON'T LIKE A TREND, JUST WAIT UNTIL IT EXPIRES AND SEEMS SILLY: Maya said it: "Every storm runs out of rain." Thankfully, every trend eventually runs out of steam, which was the case with Anne, Gilbert, Christine, and the Remembered Philopena.

In a delectable scene in *Anne of Ingleside*, Anne jealously watches a reunion between Gilbert and his ex-girlfriend, and we are stopped short by a reference to "philopenas." We definitely had to look that up, but before we share our findings, let's set the stage:

Anne, who is middle aged, is feeling frumpy and neglected by an oddly absentminded Gilbert. She really feels neglected when Gilbert agrees to meet up with his ex, Christine Stuart—the following Tuesday—his and Anne's anniversary! (Oh, Gilbert....And here we thought you were the perfect man.)

When the day arrives, Anne stumbles into the room tripping over a bearskin rug, and the erstwhile Christine descends upon the stairs, glamorous, well-preserved, and positively brimming with nostalgic reminiscences from her long ago, barely-there, relationship with Gilbert. Poor Anne is withering inside though our heroine holds her head high.

Then a guest named Dr. Murray brings up the "p" word:

"'Does anybody ever eat philopenas now?' asked Dr. Murray, who had just cracked a twin almond. Christine turned to Gilbert.

'Do you remember that philopena we ate once?' she asked.

'Do you suppose I could forget it?' asked Gilbert."

(Gilbert, if we may say so, there's no need to have *quite* so acute a memory when it comes to one's ex-girlfriend!)

Anne wonders, "'Did a significant look pass between them?'"

When we found out what a philopena was, we better understood Anne's fears.

From Wordnik.com: A "Philopena" is a game in which a person, on finding a double-kernelled almond or nut, may offer the second kernel to another person and demand a playful forfeit from that person to be paid on their next meeting...Philopenas were often played as a form of flirtation."

As trends go, the Philopena had already faded out like a pinafore hung out to dry in the sun, which meant that Christine sounded fatuous, on top of inappropriate. In the end, it was really a win for Anne, and

Gilbert, as readers know. Read all about it in *Anne of Ingleside*. Let's just say Gilbert Blythe does not disappoint.

⬤ SHRIMP WIGGLE: Trendy food is not always a good idea: In *Emily of Deep Valley* by Maud Hart Lovelace, Emily Webster felt the lure of the modish eatables of her day, none of which she knew how to make. Sure, all the other girls in town would serve vogueish vittles such as "shrimp wiggle" at their graduation parties, but the whole idea intimidated Emily.

What *is* a shrimp wiggle? Apparently, this old food fad was essentially creamed shrimp with peas on toast, kind of like Welsh Rarebit or chipped beef. You made a roux out of butter and cream, mixed in some shrimp and peas, and glopped it onto toast points. It was a popular thing for coeds to make in chafing dishes at their dorms, kind of like the ramen noodles of its day.

"I had no idea what exactly shrimp wiggle was, but the name, to me, was absolutely delightful," writes Aimee Levitt in an article about shrimp wiggle. "It conjured up images of happy 1920s ladies driving around in roadsters, their bobbed hair waving in the breeze, and someone named Mildred hanging onto her hat as she bounces in the rumble seat."

Cheery though it may sound, attempting shrimp wiggle, for Emily, would have been a mistake, just as it would be for any one of us to try and make a trendy food, just because it's trendy. So Emily did not, instead opting to cook dishes she felt comfortable making. (Read about her resounding success in Chapter 3!)

HEROINE CHALLENGE

EAT FOODS THAT SPARK YOUR INTEREST

What were the books that kept you turning the pages growing up? The dog-eared paperbacks you took with you to dentist appointments or the one book that made you feel seen? We're talking pure nostalgia here. Maybe it was the *Baby-Sitters Club, Nancy Drew, American Girl,* or the *Boxcar Mysteries.* Was there a food item or meal you remember intriguing you?

Whatever it may be, find a way to incorporate a literary food reference from your past into your next hospitable engagement. Maybe you serve a tomato sandwich á la *Harriet the Spy* to your friend who's coming over for lunch, or a bowl of yogurt-covered raisins (Baby-Sitters Club meeting style) along with the decaf at your next book club. Use this blast from the past to spark your own curiosity and a new conversation with your friend—what are the books that shaped her? Are there any foods she was obsessed with growing up, literary or otherwise?

MARZIPAN HEDGEHOG

Are you looking for the perfect non-savory side dish or dessert for your next fancy dinner party? You have likely come across a plethora of options, but they all lack *je ne sais quoi*.

We present the marzipan hedgehog.

It pairs well with everything, mainly because it actually complements nothing. With its nutty almond base, subtle floral undertones, and sweet and creamy surroundings, your guests will never forget this unusual confection, and not just because the gummy residue will remain on their teeth long after they depart.

FOR THE MARZIPAN, YOU WILL NEED

½ lb. finely ground almonds or almond flour

1 tsp. orange flower water

1 whole egg, 2 yolks

½ C sugar (or more if desired)

½ C cream

¼ C butter, melted

slivered almonds for spines

currants or raisins for eyes

FOR THE CUSTARD

1 C cream

2 egg yolks

¼ C sugar

1. Put the ground almonds, orange flower water, egg and yolks, sugar, cream, and melted butter in a metal bowl and stir together until it forms a paste.

2. Place the metal bowl over a saucepan full of water and heat over medium-low heat. Stir the mixture until it becomes thick enough to shape, about 20-25 minutes.

3. Remove from heat and let cool slightly until cold enough to handle. Shape into the form of a hedgehog and decorate with almond slivers for spines. Use currants or raisins for the eyes and nose.

4. To make the custard, heat the cream, egg yolks, and sugar in a double boiler or in a metal bowl placed over a saucepan full of water. Keep stirring until it thickens slightly, about 15 minutes. Pour around the hedgehog. Place it in the fridge until the custard is set. Just before serving, give it a proper British name.

REGENCY ERA MARZIPAN hedgehog

FOOD is a touchstone to the PAST, AND A pathway TO THE HOME and HISTORY we all carry inside.

ZORA

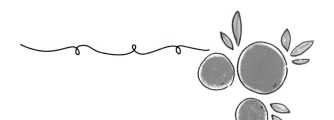

Chapter 10

BOND WITH YOUR HERITAGE LIKE A HEROINE

HOLD, KEEP, AND RECREATE ALL THE RECIPES, CUSTOMS, AND CULTURAL GEMS

"When my mom stood over these pots of spicy and earth-colored broth I knew she was remembering. Her mind was elsewhere, and memories I didn't know or understand were being stirred up alongside the softened vegetables."

TASHA JUN, *TELL ME THE DREAM AGAIN*

PROBLEM: We feel disconnected from our ethnic heritage, cultural traditions, and even our cherished family members who have passed on. We want to gain meaning and connection to these important things and people, but don't know how.

HEROINE SOLUTIONS: The heroines show us how to rediscover or deepen our discovery of our ethnic and cultural heritage, and how to get to know and even spend time with our beloved, essential people now gone through their food traditions and recipes.

For Esperanza Ortega, the stickiness, smell, and taste of mangoes would always be linked to memories of her beloved papa, who bought her a flower-shaped mango treat when she was small. That's the way it is with food—it attaches us to our families, cultures, and ourselves like nothing else. The act of whipping up a batch of waffles with the oddball yet delectable "Mennonite White Sauce" enfolds Lorilee in her Mennonite heritage. For Jenny, tasting thickly iced "Sour Cream Softies" cookies at family Christmas gatherings is a meaningful connection to a grandma she never truly got to know.

Do you, as we do, long to connect to your heritage? As always, Esperanza, Anne, Zora, et al. show the way. Whether it be a secret recipe passed down, a cultural dish laden with meaning, or a long-ago instruction for making butter beans, the heroines show us how food stirs memory, birthright, and belonging. In their kitchens and at their cookstoves, they demonstrate how food is a touchstone to the past, and a pathway to the home and history we all carry inside.

ESPERANZA & THE SCENT OF GUAVA

Esperanza remembers a special train trip with her Papa and her friend, Miguel, when they were small. "When they arrived in Zacatecas, a woman wrapped in a colorful rebozo, a blanket shawl, boarded the train selling mangoes on a stick. The mangoes were peeled and carved to look like exotic flowers. Papa bought one for each of them. On the return ride, she and Miguel, with their noses pressed against the window, and their hands still sticky from the fresh mango, had waved to every person they saw."

Later, when her Papa is dead and she and her mother are fleeing Mexico, lying under a pile of guavas in a truck, Esperanza's memories are stirred by the scent and she feels her late father's devotion and strength, just for a moment.

There was a study a few years ago that proves that the sense of smell evokes memory and emotion like nothing else. Swedes, whose average age was seventy-five, were offered three different sets of the same twenty memory cues—the prompt as a word, as a picture, and as a smell. The scientists found that while the word and visual cues provoked memories largely from their adolescence and young adulthood, the smell cues brought them all the way back to childhood.

The elderly Swedish folks described these old memories in lush, emotional fashion, reporting the feeling of being brought back in time. They smelled spices and they were in the kitchen, making *Pepparkakor* with Aunt Greta. They smelled fresh mown grass and they were transported to long ago summer days.

We would be at a loss to explain the brain science, but the sense of smell triggers memory and emotion in a way that leaves the other four senses in the dust. A 2008 *New York Times* piece called the nose "an emotional time machine."

Food scents, such as the gingersnaps your mom always made for Christmas, or roast beef baking in an oven at grandma's house, can bring back memories of loved ones and times gone by in a way that nothing else can.

In Lorilee's 2015 book *Anne of Green Gables, My Daughter, and Me,* she remembers the aromas of her childhood kitchen:

"The kitchen smelled of bay leaves and cabbage, of rhubarb and plums and canning spices, their shared tradition and heritage, 443 years of Mennonite foods and folkways expressed in a kettle of borscht and fruit Platz with streusel topping."

And in one scented swoop, those smells tied her to both her loved ones and the Mennonite culture in which she was immersed.

MENNONITE WHITE SAUCE & OTHER FOODS AND FOLKWAYS OF LORILEE'S HERITAGE

Nothing takes me back to the haven of my Mennonite grandmother's farm kitchen like the smell of moist and flavorful roast beef cooking, except maybe the buttery spice of her ginger snaps. There was always something divine cooking or baking at grandma's little house on the prairie.

Years later, while interviewing Amish folk for my book *Money Secrets of the Amish*, I found myself transported back to grandma's farm, with the scents of Amish cooking triggering memories (it was suddenly a no-brainer to dedicate my Amish book to Grandma Loewen). I remembered that, at my grandma's table, she used to wait a few minutes for her loved ones to start eating her delicious food. "*Schmeckt gut, yo?*" she would ask, her merry brown eyes twinkling. And the answer was always "*Yo!*" Everything always tasted as good as it smelled.

I was also surprised to find that, though Mennonites and Amish split up in 1693 over the scandalous matter of buttons, there were still connections between my culture and theirs.

Food was definitely a bond, as echoes of the breads, tortes, and preserves of their common European past showed up on both Mennonite and Amish tables. Everywhere these two people groups traveled, they made a garden out of the wilderness with bone-hard work and ingenuity learned from their traditions.

The pleasure of eating runs through each culture, for necessity and for social gatherings. From Lancaster County, PA to the Manitoba prairies, from the Ukrainian fruit orchards to the Paraguayan Chaco, the food traditions of the Amish and the Mennonites have flourished.

Some of my earliest memories revolve around the foods of my culture. An old black and white photo shows my dad's family seated around a table laden with Mennonite food: Bowls of Pluma Moos (cold fruit soup) and borscht, serving dishes heaped with wareniki (pierogies), farmer sausage, and fleish perishke (meat buns).

I would always pass on Pluma Moos, which featured skinned plums, bobbing in a milky, Gazpacho-like chilled soup. Because the *Moos* part of it was pronounced "mouse," for the life of me, I couldn't disassociate it with floating dead mice.

Borscht, a rendition of the soup we picked up during our one hundred fifty years living in Ukraine, my dad's birthplace, is also not my favorite. Traditional Mennonite borscht calls for everything but the kitchen sink (soup bones, potatoes, onions, bay leaves, peppercorns, aniseed, heavy cream, tomatoes…I could go on). It also calls for copious amounts of cabbage to be shredded by hand while the cook hums along to mournful German hymns and listens to "The Hog Report" on a radio station being piped out of the prairies.

I have turned my back on this rendition, which is too complicated and oniony for my tastes. My adult version of that famous soup of Eastern European immigrants is a dump-and-stir recipe using the slow cooker and utilizing beets, favored by Ukrainians and Polish in their kettles of borscht. Personally, I like beets a whole lot more than cabbage, although there's some of that in this recipe too.

The best thing about my borscht is it takes five minutes, if you do it the lazy way, and I do. My recipe calls for cans of diced beets, undrained (If you buy Amish canned beets at a roadside stand, people become even more inordinately impressed. This also makes it a tad more Mennonite); cans of beef broth, dehydrated onions (just to appease the onion fans), pre-shredded cabbage, sugar, and lemon juice, with delicious swishes of sour cream and dill sprinkled on to taste.

The color changes from beet red, literally, to Pepto Bismol pink, depending on how many glops of sour cream you stir in. Guests have been inordinately impressed with the fact that I made borscht, and don't we all want to impress our guests inordinately? The key is to humbly utter, "Thank you," while not making eye contact with my husband, who knows it took me five minutes. This takes some practice—the humble response, not the soup.

Though I'm a bona-fide Mennonite from the prairies, I'm just too much of a city slicker softie to butcher pigs, bring in the sheaves, or, as my Oma did when she was in her forties, build her own oven in the Paraguayan jungle, making hundreds of mud bricks by hand. This girl needs her shortcuts and all the hacks.

While I was able to find a great hack for borscht and a nifty recipe for bread machine Paska (Ukrainian Easter Bread), other Mennonite foods seem to be quite un-hackable. Take fleish perishke, or Menno Meat Buns. These little pillows of bun dough stuffed with spiced meat are absolutely delectable, not to mention manifold in ingredients and steps. My friend's grandma used to have a business making and selling these savory bonbons out of her kitchen. God bless Bonnie's grandma, in Heaven now, making fleish perishke for the angels.

My dad, Abe the Bookseller, loved his meat buns; although, if you met my dad even once it was clear he did not like to miss a meal of any kind. He cherished all the Mennonite beige foods—pierogies with *schmaunt fat* (creamy gravy), *koteletten* potato salad, and plum *platz* with the plums hidden under layers of golden strudel topping. But his favorite beige food was Napoleon Torte, also borrowed from Ukraine, who borrowed it from Russia vis-à-vis France, where it is known as *mille-feuille*.

No birthday or New Year's celebration was complete without a slice of this pudding pylon, twelve layers deep of custard and pastry. My mom learned to make it decently, but no one could scaffold those spongy layers like my Tante Susie, his big sister. When I moved to Michigan, I found myself only five hours from my aunt, from whom I learned more about my dad's story, especially the hidden layers I sensed were there from his wartime childhood. For me, my family's history is incomplete without talking about food.

Food and story. Story and food. They go together like *varenike* and *schmaunt* fat, or waffles and Mennonite White Sauce.

Mennonite *What* Sauce? It's one of the more bluntly named yet peculiar foods of my people—a runny, warm, vanilla custard sauce, just the thing to pour over waffles on a frosty day. Passed down from Holland to Belgium to Russia and then to immigrants in a new land, this humble though decadent sauce is known to all Mennonites but is a culinary mystery to "Englishers." (See recipe at the end of chapter.) It's just one more taste that moors me to the culture and people group who are such a big part of my identity.

JENNY'S GERMAN HERITAGE & THE COOKIE THAT SLIPPED THROUGH THE CRACKS

I recently read for the first time a book that has been on the shelf of my family's library for many years. It is a thin teal green paperback, and on the cover is a blurry black and white photograph of a man wearing a hat standing next to a horse. The book is called *This Is My Life,* and it is written by John Bockmann, my great-grandfather. Only a handful of physical copies exist in the world because it was never meant to be read by anyone outside of his own posterity. Originally written by hand, the manuscript was typed and bound after he died, and a copy was given to each of his children and grandchildren.

I had known about this book since I was a young child, and I remember trying to read it as a teenager but not getting past the first few pages. Maybe I thought I had heard from my dad all the stories there were to know.

I knew, for instance, he was eight years old in 1905 when his family came to America on a boat from Germany and settled in Nebraska. The stories of his inventions were legendary to my siblings and me, who would groan loudly over the injustice we vicariously felt every time our dad told us how his patent for the first-ever corn husker machine was copied by a large farm equipment manufacturer. "We could have been rich!" we'd say, even though we weren't really mourning the loss of our imaginary inheritance. We were simply proud to have descended from such an interesting man. And knowing these stories were *the inheritance,* you can bet we were going to make the most of them.

His daughter, Fern, was my grandma, and despite visiting her on a annual basis as a young girl, I never knew her well because of her early onset Alzheimer's Disease. What I would give for an autobiography of her life! But while I don't have her stories, I do have her sour cream softies recipe, her white china teacups, and the shape of her face.

There were many more stories I had not heard, however. Like the one where he and his little sister wandered from home and almost died in quicksand, saved at the final hour by a man who decided on a whim to take a meandering route on his way home. If it weren't for that stranger, I wouldn't be pouring tea into china teacups for my own botanically named daughters and asking, "Do you remember who these belonged to?" (They know, they assure me, and think the ritual a wondrous thing.)

Every Christmas as a child, my mouth watered as I laid eyes on the sour cream softies my aunt brought to our holiday gatherings. These cloud-like cookies fairly glistened in their colorfully iced coats, layered between sheets of parchment paper in unassuming Tupperware containers. She brought them because her mom (Grandma Fern) made them, and her mom before her. Now, my sister has carried on the tradition and, every year, our collective memories are strengthened over a particular scent, flavor, and texture on our taste buds. I take a bite and remember the way I'd sit close to my grandma as a little girl, listening to her hum a favorite hymn while gazing steadily into the distance, wishing she would turn her head and know my name. While I never *really* knew my grandma, I do know we both adore Jane Eyre, and we have the same favorite cookie. And really, that was only the beginning of what we shared.

Recently, I asked my dad why he didn't eat more food from his German heritage growing up. And my mom, why she grew up eating casseroles instead of recipes passed on from her mom's mom. For both of my parents, *their* parents were cooking the food of their generation: frozen, canned, and processed foods were new and all the rage, and highly convenient for feeding both of their large families. But the cookie, I just recently learned, has German origins, and it slipped through the cracks of the changing times. It remains as the singular flavor that binds us to our European heritage.

If I've learned anything from an unremarkable tea set and a very sweet (but oh so light, fluffy, and melt-in-your-mouth) cookie, it's that it doesn't take much to feel connected to the people whose existence led to your own. And even a small reminder (the size of a cookie crumb) that we were all born of the sacrifices of others is a little bit like looking up at the stars: it quickly puts our Very Important and Individual Lives into perspective.

I'll make sure my children get the German sour cream softies recipe, of course, but I'll also give them my mom's recipe for the potato crescent rolls we eat every holiday season, and my ginger molasses cookie recipe too. And along with my grandpa's book, they'll get a new accumulation of stories from *their* grandparents.

The good thing about reading your great-grandpa's book in your thirties is that it serves as a reminder that it is never too late to connect to your family's history on a deeper level. And if you don't know much about the people and recipes that came before you, or if the foods that make you think of them don't excite you, then you can choose to be a tide-turner like my mom, and start sharing the recipes that you love most, simply because you think they are delicious, with the people you love. What a beautiful inheritance to leave for the ones who come after you, these edible stories that pass effortlessly through generations, that are as theoretically accessible as the kitchen, and the closest thing to your grandma's embrace.

 ## HEROINE TAKEAWAYS

- **FOOD BINDS US TO OUR CULTURAL AND ETHNIC HERITAGE:** In Zora Neale Hurston's novel *Their Eyes Were Watching God*, our heroine Janie returns from the Everglades to Eatonville in frayed overalls to a judgy and cold town. Only her best friend Phoeby, welcomes her, bringing Janie a "heaping plate of mulatto rice." Janie tucks into the simple, heartening meal, even as Phoeby remarks that it "ain't so good dis time. Not enough bacon grease." She does however admit that "it'll kill hongry." This generous offering not only killed hungry, but also loneliness. Janie had Phoeby in her corner, and that was enough.

Later in the novel, her great love Tea Cake's willingness to cook for Janie sets him apart from other men in her life. According to Frederick Douglass Opie, historian and author of *Zora Neale Hurston on Florida Food*, those foodie scenes showed Hurston's keen interest in how food and social traditions intersected.

Food such as mulatto rice, sugarcane-sweetened lemonade, and barbecued chicken and pork was a recurring theme in Zora's writings, both in her work as a novelist and as an anthropologist. She knew that food is a prime way to connect to one's culture and region.

Opie quotes from Hurston's "Folklore" of her love for Florida cooking, and her cheeky musings of these comfort foods while men unsuccessfully flirted with her: "I sometimes feel the divine urge [for love] for an hour, a day, or maybe a week. Then it is gone and my interest returns to corn pone [pudding] and mustard greens."

At one point in her life, she made ends meet by selling Florida-style chicken (which was grilled, not fried) out of the shared kitchen of her Harlem boarding house. She'd also bake coconut layer cakes as thank-yous to supporters like the Barnard trustee who secured her scholarship.

As an anthropologist, she embedded herself in all kinds of places to watch and learn about people. The General Store featured huge bottles of pickled pigs's feet, then a romantic token of courting. There were also specific foods at the juke joint, one of Zora's places to observe the culture. "Fried chicken, fried gator, barbeque pork, and unbelievable moonshine," said Opie in an interview with the podcast *Good Food*. She would also attend large community barbecues, where whole hogs would be barbecued over an open pit of pecan, apple, and hickory wood. All of these food-related experiences nourished her with not just calories but a deepened attachment with her heritage as a Black woman living in the Deep South, specifically Florida.

Zora understood that food nurtured both body and soul, that it was our best teacher to impart lessons about our own ethnic and cultural background and those of others. She would have said "Amen" to the late Anthony Bourdain, who grasped in a beautiful way how food ties us to our roots like nothing else. "Food is everything we are," he said. "It's an extension of nationalist feeling, ethnic feeling, your personal history, your province, your region, your tribe, your grandma. It's inseparable from those from the get-go."

Yes, Mr. Bourdain. Food is an extension of one's country and ethnicity. It is at the center of all cultures and family gatherings. We, like our best-loved authors and book characters, experience many of our biggest moments in life either preparing or sharing a meal.

We'll let the heroines speak for themselves:

Esperanza Ortega: "It wasn't exactly like the birthdays of her past, but it would still be a celebration, under the china and mulberry trees, with newborn rosebuds from Papa's garden. Although there were no papayas, there was cantaloupe, lime, and coconut salad. And *machaca burritos* topped with lots of love and laughter and teasing. At the end of the meal, Josefina brought out a *flan de almendras*, Esperanza's favorite, and they sang the birthday song to her again" (*Esperanza Rising*).

Patria Mirabel: "My mouth, for instance, craved sweets, figs in their heavy syrup, coconut candy, soft, golden flans" (*In the Time of the Butterflies* by Julia Alvarez).

Attributed to Maya Angelou: "The best comfort food will always be greens, cornbread, and fried chicken."

Jing-Mei Woo: "Time to eat," Auntie An-mei happily announces, bringing out a steaming pot of wonton she was just wrapping. There are piles of food on the table, served buffet style. Just like at the Kweilin feasts…The wonton soup smells wonderful with delicate sprigs of cilantro floating on top. I'm drawn first to the large platter of chaswei, sweet barbequed pork cut into coin sized slices, and then to a whole assortment of what I've always called finger goodies—thin-skinned pastries filled with chopped pork, beef, shrimp, and unknown stuffings that my mother used to describe as "nutritious things" (*The Joy Luck Club* by Amy Tan).

⬤ FOOD BINDS US TO FAMILY AND FRIENDS: One of the best ways to connect to a lost loved one is to make a food that reminds us of them. Even better, to make it the way they taught us.

In *Roll of Thunder, Hear My Cry*, Cassie Logan's mama showed her how to churn butter. When the butter was ready, she said: "Dip out the butter like I showed you and wash it down. I'll take care of the milk…I scooped the butter from the churning lid onto a plate and went through the curtain to the small pantry off the kitchen to get the molding dish."

One another occasion, Cassie was in the kitchen, talking to her mother and measuring flour for the cornbread they were fixing for supper. "Only one tablespoon, Cassie, and not so heaping," her mother instructed her. They were running low on flour, and Mrs. Logan was teaching her daughter how to cook and conserve at the same time. She then modeled how to stir milk into the butter beans, a major component of the meal they were preparing, of cornbread and butter beans.

Countless home cooks have learned how to prepare special foods through watching beloved family members, whether it be a mother, grandmother, father, or grandfather. Nothing ties us to our families like a particular food we associate with them. Especially when these family members are no longer living, making and eating these foods is one of the most significant ways we can keep their memories alive. Lorilee's daughter Phoebe just had her graduation open house, where they served up Grandpa Craker's white chili and Grandma Craker's Mexican chef salad (not Mexican *at all*, but tasty!). Grandpa has been gone for six years, but they were pretty sure he was in that cloud of witnesses, grinning whenever someone asked for the recipe.

Which dish do you think of when you think of your mother, grandmother, or another cherished family member or friend? Did you, like Cassie, learn to make it from them?

Whether it be a specific dish or a food-related tradition, our heroines show us how food binds us to the past and makes us feel closer to those we carry in our hearts.

⬤ RECIPES CAN BE LOVING LEGACIES: "I get out mother's old cookbook and read the doughnut recipe—and the other recipes," said Cecilia Meredith in *Rainbow Valley*, the seventh book in the *Anne of Green Gables* series.

For Cecilia, reading her late mother's old cookbook was comforting, a way to remember and even reach for her in spirit.

In *Emily of Deep Valley*, Emily Webster also learns more about the mother she hardly knew through her recipe for frog's legs. When Emily tells her grandfather and guardian that they are going to have frog legs (sold to her by some enterprising boys from the town's Syrian community) for supper, she is surprised at his response.

"They're good," he says. "Your mother used to fix them."

Astounded, Emily is launched on a mission of discovery "through old cook books, unfolding yellowed papers on which recipes had been written at long-gone thimble bees, tea parties and Ladies Aid meetings."

Finally, she finds her mother's handwritten recipe, and eventually, Emily becomes so good at making frogs's legs, she ends up making this dish for her friends, confident in her mother's cooking help across time and eternity.

When a recipe or beloved food is handed down from one generation to another—or maybe even one friend to another—it becomes more than nourishment. It becomes a bequest of banana bread, a legacy of lemon meringue pie, a heritage of ham hocks.

Of course, not every recipe is recorded for posterity. Lorilee's grandma never wrote any of them down at all, and that's not uncommon for cooks of yore. So many heirloom recipes only really existed in people's heads and hearts.

In her *New York Times* review of the novel *Black Cake* by Charmaine Wilkerson, Elisabeth Egan wrote that as she read, "I kept looking forward to the recipe for black cake. I was sure it would appear at the back of the book." But when Benny (who dreams of opening her own cafe) finally finds her mother's recipe tucked away in a junk drawer, "it has no numbers, no quantities at all." She realizes it "was never so much a list of firm quantities and instructions as a series of hints for how to proceed."

Isn't this the case with many treasured dishes?

Yet sometimes our inheritance may not be in a written recipe, but in the stories and memories that arise when we attempt to make a loved one's signature dish. Even when we use modern methods and shortcuts to craft those old dishes, it still counts. The memories and stories still shimmer, and the ties that bind us to our heritage become stronger each time we make them.

HEROINE CHALLENGE
ASK YOUR FAMILY

Ask your parents or other family members what recipes connect them to loved ones now gone. Or, if you have kids that are older, ask them what recipes connect them to memories of family. Whether or not you feel your food heritage is strong, consider making a recipe this week that makes you feel connected to someone you love, and in turn, share it with the people you love! If you are looking for bonus points, gather all the recipes you'd consider to be part of your family history and compile them into one place for safekeeping (even if that's just a bookmarked page on your laptop).

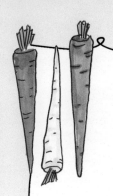

Recipes

LORILEE'S MENNONITE WHITE SAUCE

Recently, a non-Mennonite friend who had attended a Mennonite high school told me she had wondered for twenty-five years what exactly was *in* Mennonite White Sauce; she had enjoyed it tremendously as a guest in friends's homes.

Wonder no more, Heather W. This recipe solves the mystery. Enjoy this sauce with light and fluffy waffles, by itself, or with any fruit topping:

MENNONITE WHITE SAUCE FOR WAFFLES

INGREDIENTS

2 C milk

1 Tbsp. cornstarch

1½ C sugar (some recipes call for as little as 2 Tbsp. of sugar, so you can play with how sweet you'd like it)

1 tsp. vanilla extract

2 eggs, beaten

INSTRUCTIONS

1. Let the milk boil.

2. Mix sugar and cornstarch.

3. Add to eggs and mix into milk, stirring until thick.

4. At the end, add the vanilla.

GRANDMA FERN'S SOUR CREAM SOFTIES

INGREDIENTS

½ C unsalted butter, softened
1 C sugar
1 egg
1 tsp. pure vanilla extract
½ C sour cream

MIX TOGETHER THESE AND SET ASIDE

3 ¼ C flour
1 tsp. baking soda
½ tsp. salt

FOR THE FROSTING

6 Tbsp. unsalted butter, softened
1 lb. powdered sugar
¼ C milk
1 ½ tsp. pure vanilla extract

INSTRUCTIONS

1. Beat together butter, sugar, egg, and vanilla on high speed of an electric mixer for two minutes, scraping bowl as needed.

2. Add the sour cream and mix.

3. Add flour mixture and beat on low until well-blended. Dough will be very soft.

4. Roll out onto a lightly floured surface, ¼ inch thick. Cut into desired shapes with cookie cutters and place on parchment lined pan.

5. Bake at 350 degrees F (177 C) for 10-12 minutes until bottoms are just barely golden brown.

(continues on next page)

FOR THE FROSTING

1. Beat butter in an electric mixer until smooth.

2. Add powdered sugar, milk, and vanilla and beat until smooth.

3. Spread onto cooled cookies.

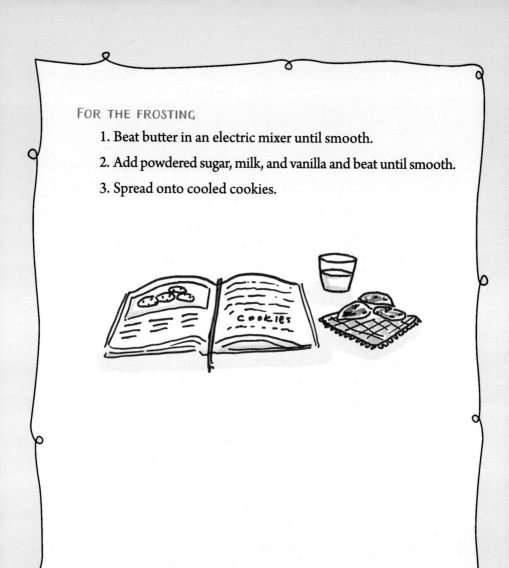

What are some of the food traditions and recipes from your heritage?

"Next to TRYING and WINNING, the best THING is trying AND FAILING."

—ANNE OF GREEN GABLES

Chapter 11

REDEEM FOOD SCRAPES & DISASTERS LIKE A HEROINE

STARRING ANNE OF GREEN GABLES AND THE MOUSE WHO PERISHED IN HER PLUM PUDDING

"Tomorrow is a new day with no mistakes in it yet."
ANNE OF GREEN GABLES

PROBLEM: Despite owning ovens with knobs, we are not immune to the occasional culinary embarrassment or hospitality faux pas. Kitchen catastrophes happen to the best of us, so how can we respond with grace and good humor?

HEROINE SOLUTION: The heroines remind us that culinary disasters and disappointments do occur—even in fiction—with depressing regularity. Although these mishaps might be more entertaining in literature, the heroines teach us that food has the power to heal wounded hearts (in the form of "humble pie" perhaps), make friends out of strangers, and give us the opportunity to rise gracefully above our sauce shortcomings and kitchen catastrophes. And if all else fails, we remind you of what Nora Ephron's mother used to tell her, "Everything is copy, everything is material, someday you will think this is funny."

If being a good cook is next to godliness in Avonlea, Anne Shirley is a long way off from culinary heaven. But she has plenty to teach us about recovering from kitchen disasters. She teaches us that whether you set your bosom friend drunk on "raspberry cordial," come close to serving your favorite teacher a dessert marinated in drowned rodent, or flavor the cake with a liquid pain reliever, redemption exists. We read vignettes of our heroines burning food, botching meals, and over-sugaring the peas (Anne, again), yet we also absorb the valuable heart knowledge that redemption is possible.

Anne, along with others, has plenty to teach us about recovering from kitchen disasters. As in cooking and life in general, we relish in Anne's heroic mindset that, "Tomorrow is a new day with no mistakes in it yet."

When we read about the foibles of our heroines, we are entertained without a great deal of vicarious embarrassment, and we accept the valleys our heroines must pass through because this is a story, after all, and our beloved characters couldn't grow and thrive if they were merely skipping merrily from peak to peak. And yet, when such occasions happen in our own lives, we might be tempted to view them as *unfunny* and *un*necessary without the context of a front and back cover. But who can blame us? We can't see the whole story while we are still in the midst of it.

But this is exactly why we keep returning to our favorite heroine books: a good story can help us see reality more clearly, helping us make more sense of our own story, even before we reach the end.

When Amy March gathers the courage to invite her fancy school chums over for lunch, we feel her pain when only one guest shows up. But what does this do for our little Amy who struggles with a major dose of vanity? It forces her to rely on her family and, more importantly, helps her to understand that any occasion that is begun solely with the intention to impress is just begging for a lesson in humility. For Amy, this failed party is a colossal embarrassment. But thankfully, it is a humiliation from which she not only recovers, but improves!

The eldest March sister, Meg, suffers from her own mishap as a newlywed, when her dear husband spontaneously invites a friend over for dinner, giving Meg no warning. When he and his friend Mr. Scott approach the Brooke home, instead of finding his smiling queen beneath an open window, giving the last flourishes to a fine meal, John finds Meg in the kitchen, where "confusion and despair" reign, sobbing under her apron.

We speak of the Currant Jelly Catastrophe, when Meg's zeal for home canning dissolved into tears, disillusionment, and the lovebirds' first major fight.

Though her dream was that John "should fare sumptuously every day," reality hit hard when her "dainty dishes" gave John a stomachache and he insisted on meat and potatoes, or at least something basic and edible that would not render him dyspeptic.

Still, the duo were as happy as two little New England clams until Meg was suddenly possessed with the urge to make jam from the only free fruit available to them: currants, that ubiquitous heroine favorite, "Their only crop of fruit."

"Fired with a housewifely wish to see her storeroom stocked with homemade preserves, she undertook to put up her own currant jelly," Alcott writes, setting up the scene.

Somehow in this era, even the thrifty could order cuts of meat or other provisions to be sent to the home, like Instacart, but with clips of horses, not clicks on the internet. *Clip clop*—the currants are ripe! John orders four dozen little pots, half a barrel of sugar, and a little boy to pick the currants for Meg. (Perhaps we are using the wrong grocery delivery service…)

The young housewife definitely tried her best, "feeling no doubts about her success, for hadn't she seen Hannah do it hundreds of times?"

Our Meg valiantly boiled, strained, and fussed over the jelly. She consulted *The Young Housekeeper's Friend*, hoping there would be a clue to her success in its well-worn pages. Meg "racked her brain" to remember what Hannah had done, and "she reboiled, resugared, and restrained, but that dreadful stuff wouldn't 'jell.'"

She wanted to run home to Marmee for help, but she had too much pride. By five o'clock, she wept loudly among the ruby red ruins of her canning carnage. Outside, the boy who had been retained for picking lay asleep under the currant bush, smeared with bloody looking juice. It was upon this staggering image, enlivened by the pervasive smell of burned sugar, that John Brooke returned to the Dovecote (their house's nickname), and readers, he wasn't alone. Oh no, John had picked *that day* to take Meg up on her magnanimous—and totally boneheaded—offer to always feel free to bring a colleague home for supper after work—no need to even ask her beforehand!

"I'm afraid something has happened," John manages to tell his colleague, the hungry bachelor Mr. Scott.

Yes, something had happened. Confusion and despair happened. Pans running over with jelly the consistency of Kool-Aid, and Meg, an apron over her head, sobbing, happened. (Meanwhile, Lotty, the German hired girl, placidly drank currant wine, and we can't blame her.)

John begs Meg to tell him quickly what has caused her so much grief, and receives the explanation, "The…The jelly won't jell and I don't know what to do!" Here we pause to recognize that, given the importance of gelatin in the worlds of our heroines, this is nothing short of a crisis. Pollyanna, especially, would have understood this is no time to laugh—and laugh John did.

John is sympathetic at first, then embarrassed, and finally tries to make a joke that goes over about as well as the jelly.

"It's a scrape, I acknowledge, but if you will lend a hand, we'll pull through and have a good time yet…Give us the cold meat, and bread and cheese. We won't ask for jelly."

Too soon, John. *Way* too soon.

But we don't blame the man for taking her up on this genuine suggestion, nor do we blame him for vowing never to do it again.

Meg notifies John to tell Mr. Scott that she is sick or dead or *something* and runs up to her room to hide and cry. And John feeds Mr. Scott a "promiscuous lunch" whereafter the bachelor is dispatched to his home and Meg and John must face up to their sticky kitchen situation.

Jelly that does not jell is indeed the catalyst for John and Meg's first spousal spat. And while the layers of hurt and blame surrounding this incident could rival an onion's, Meg harbored some perfectionist tendencies she needed to release. And we applaud her in this scene, because in the midst of the quiet stewing between the pair later that evening, Meg remembers Marmee's advice to always "be the first to seek pardon." That is never an easy pill to swallow, but Meg does it with such grace, and with such sweeping consolations, that she and John are able to laugh about the Tragedy of the Un-Jelled Jelly for years to come.

Meg and John both had preconceived ideas of what their lives at home would look like, and Meg, unsurprisingly, raised the bar for herself quite high. But she recognized that she is human, and that her love for John was worth protecting more than her pride. What could have become a thorn in their marriage blossoms into a hilarious story, thanks to Meg's willingness to be transformed.

 ## HEROINE TAKEAWAYS

● OWN UP TO YOUR MISTAKES, LIKE ANNE SHIRLEY: Anne Shirley has plenty to teach us about recovering from kitchen disasters. She more than any heroine got herself into scrape after scrape and lived to tell the tale(s).

Anne's most famous food-related disaster was the whole "setting Diana drunk" fiasco. You remember, of course, how Anne invited Diana over for tea, and ended up stumbling out the door, totally spiffed.

Anne is allowed to offer cherry preserves, fruitcake, cookies, and snaps—not a cheese cube in sight at this soirée.

But what did they drink—besides tea? (Cue up fraught music that portends of doom.) We all know the answer—Raspberry Cordial, aka Red Currant Wine; that's what Diana drank anyway. Anne somehow mixed up the two bottles and ended up serving her eleven-year-old friend an alcoholic beverage. Iconic, to be sure.

As Diana continued to drink and drink, Anne regaled her with two stories, one of her forgetting to put flour in a cake, and one of her forgetting to cover the plum pudding sauce, whereupon a mouse drowned in it, and she fished it out with a spoon. Of course, that episode ended badly, as Anne also forgot to tell Marilla about the mouse in the sauce, and Marilla came close to serving the mouse-infused plum pudding sauce to an elegant guest. However, Anne stopped her just in time.

This vignette within a vignette teaches us that when you have made a big mistake, own up to it as soon as possible. Remember, big mistakes equal big guts to make them right. Anne did the right thing, even though it cost her.

● HANG IN THERE, HEROINE, BECAUSE SOMETIMES GRACE IS IN SHORT SUPPLY, BUT THINGS WORK OUT ANYWAY: Back to Diana drinking "tumblers" of Red Currant Wine. Diana is sick, she is dizzy, she is DRUNK. This is disastrous, as Diana's mother, the uptight and prejudiced Mrs. Barry, somehow thinks Anne—the suspicious orphan—had intentionally "set Diana drunk," and refuses to let her daughter and Anne be friends anymore.

This is catastrophic for our formerly friendless heroine, who finds herself bereft of her best friend, soon after finding her! Our poor Anne Girl is plunged into the very depth of despair and must go about her life in a sad and lonely fashion for months. This radically unjust consequence does not get corrected until the Fateful Night of Ipecac, when Anne heroically saves Diana Barry's little sister from choking to death by administering this old-fashioned expectorant.

We are not fans of this message—that you make one lousy mistake that anyone could have made, and you are not forgiven until you happen to save a kid's life! However, we are fans of Mrs. Barry groveling and eating several slices of humble pie in an attempt to absolve herself of her absurd behavior. And we are always fans of Anne doing good in the world, and her epic friendship with Diana.

Takeaway: If you have made a mistake and someone unfairly comes at you hard because of it, feel your feelings—mourn, rage, cry—and hang in there, knowing that sometimes the stiff-necked, unpleasant, and pinchy person you have inadvertently offended actually does come to her senses. And Anne is gracious. We sometimes wonder if Anne's ability to look past the mistakes of others is because she is so eager to be forgiven of her own.

● SOMETIMES, GRACE ABOUNDS: THE FAMOUS LINIMENT CAKE DEBACLE: Remember in Chapter 4, when we outlined every single thing on the menu at the fancy luncheon for Reverend Allen and his wife?

It was one item in particular where Anne committed her most serious food scrape: she accidentally poisoned the layer cake. Yes, the lovely cake, which "came out of the oven as light and feathery as golden foam." Anne "flushed with delight" and "clapped it together with layers of ruby jelly."

"All went merry as a marriage bell until Anne's layer cake was passed."
Uh oh.

Sweet Mrs. Allan is about to fall off her chair, she is so full, but because Anne had made the cake especially for them, she accepts a "plump triangle."

She takes her first bite, and the most peculiar expression crosses her face. She keeps eating because she is an angel.

Marilla notices this, and takes a bite of her own. (Presumably, Reverend Allen was having a dramatic episode of dyspepsia, having eaten enough for ten people.)

Dyspepsia: "Upper abdominal discomfort, described as burning sensation, bloating or gassiness, nausea, or feeling full too quickly after starting to eat."

The situation unfolds quickly. Marilla eats the cake and realizes it tastes like, well, liquid pain reliever. "Mercy on us, Anne, you've flavored that cake with anodyne liniment. I broke the liniment bottle last week and poured what was left into an old empty vanilla bottle. I suppose it's partly my fault—I should have warned you—but for pity's sake why couldn't you have smelled it?"

Another case of mixed-up bottles, and another humiliating cooking calamity where Anne ends up embarrassed and upset.

In her piece "What's Making Anne of Green Gables Turn Green?", Esther Inglis-Arkell researches the ingredients in Anne's failed flavoring. "Some sources say its main ingredient was ether, which says enough about the Cuthbert household. Other sources get a little more specific, and more worrying…18.5% alcohol, 6.25% ether, and half a grain of opium to the fluid ounce."

Ether and Opium? Sweet molasses, it just keeps getting worse.

However, this near-poisoning debacle was Mrs. Allan's shining moment. Every mistake leads to a choice—will the offended one choose resentment or compassion? Depending on the choice, both the offended and the offender will be taken down the road to condemnation or the road to grace. Thankfully for Anne, the minister's wife is a frequent traveler down the latter.

Everyone should have a Mrs. Allan in their lives, someone who accepts our broken offerings and believes in us anyway. She pursues Anne when she runs away in shame and disgrace. She follows her, listens with a heart full of mercy, and regards Anne's devastated face with deep concern.

We lean forward as Mrs. Allan guides Anne in repair: "Now, you mustn't cry any more, but come down with me and show me your flower garden…." She helps Anne move on, which can be the greatest medicine, liniment, for a sore spirit.

Sometimes there is grace, and Anne shows us how to lean into it with all you have. Feel all the feelings—embarrassment, shame, heartbreak—and then press into healing and a new beginning.

- EMBRACE THE "COMICAL SIDE OF THE AFFAIR": Nora Ephron's mother was right: "Everything is copy, everything is material, someday you will think this is funny." Sometimes our most mortifying moments can be transformed into good, and even hilarious, stories. Of course, a sense of humor is necessary for this to happen. Luckily, Jo March was eventually able to see the funny side of things when a dinner she made went horribly wrong and turned into a "standing joke."

We find her and her sisters experimenting with doing no housework or kitchen prep work at the outset of their summer vacation. Somehow, Jo "with perfect faith in her own powers," thinks it's a great time to invite Laurie, the boy next door, to dinner.

Meg cautions her, but Jo is dismissive. It will all come together in a snap, she thinks. Been there, how about you?

But the kitchen was a disaster, and the stove needed tending to get hot enough to cook on, and by the time Jo dealt with all of this, *she* was a hot mess. "She didn't have the expertise or experience to match her vision," say Bergstrom and Osada in *The Little Women Cookbook*.

Things were already falling apart when the sharp-nosed, gossipy old spinster Miss Crocker picked that moment to sail in and invite herself to dinner.

"Despair seized them," we are told. "Language cannot describe the anxieties, experiences, and exertions which Jo underwent that morning."

Jo plunged in, discovering that she had way overshot her cooking skills. Everything turned out all wrong.

Her saving grace, though, *could* have been the fruit, because "she had sugared it well." Everyone seated at the table was anxious to put the terrible dinner behind them—the woody asparagus, incinerated bread, fragments of lobster, and bumpy blancmange.

But no, she didn't *sugar* it at all. Her sister's diagnosis: "'Salt instead of sugar, and the cream is sour,' replied Meg with a tragic gesture." Salted fruit, then, for dessert, was just the pitiful ending this train wreck of a tuck-in deserved.

Poor Jo turned the color of a lobster and was on the very cusp of tears when she caught Laurie's twinkling eye. "The comical side of the affair suddenly struck her, and she laughed till the tears ran down her cheeks. So did everyone else, even 'Croaker' as the girls called the old lady, and the unfortunate dinner ended gaily, with bread and butter, olives and fun."

We feel your pain, Jo! But we also love you for laughing at yourself—eventually. Hey, if you can even make the Croakers of this world laugh, you know you've got a good story on your hands. Next time you overestimate your kitchen skills big time, and it ends in disaster, remember, someday this, too, could be your version of a standing joke.

A HEROINE'S TRANSFORMATION

What makes a heroine an actual heroine? Not her stalwart virtues or her superior talents, but simply this: her willingness to be transformed. This willingness comes with a great deal of vulnerability. But if vulnerability is necessary to being a heroine, then—and here we pose the question behind the creation of this book—what better way to make ourselves available to a heroine transformation than to *eat* like one?

That is, what better way to make ourselves vulnerable to transformation than by making a commitment to cooking, serving, and feasting with others? What better way to welcome someone than to invite them into our homes and share our most vulnerable spaces? It is here they will see the realness of our lives. Our guests might discover, for instance, that we make soup only from a can, that we don't vacuum under the couch, or that we splurge on the floral centerpiece but skimp on dessert. They might judge us. They might love us. Maybe they'll leave and you'll worry if they had a good time. Or maybe you'll be certain they had a good time, but you spent the evening making sure your guests had enough wine to mask the fact that the chicken tasted like cardboard. You might be hurt, you might be embarrassed, you might fail in front of everyone.

But this is what Anne, Zora, et al., in their tightly crafted heroine journeys, can teach us: One meal, one dinner party, one picnic…is not indicative of all the rest, good or bad. Anne would probably say that this makes the world more interesting. And we'd have to agree. To paraphrase Maya Angelou, "You may not control all the events that happen to you, but you can decide not to be reduced by them."

Cooking, eating, preparing, feasting, togetherness…these are all perfect conditions for building a community that supports openness and vulnerability, which leads to acceptance and love, and paves the way for making heroines (and heroes) of us all.

Lest we forget, Mrs. Lynde—prejudiced, nosey, narrow-minded Mrs. Lynde—was changed by a vulnerable orphan with an open heart in the context of a close-knit community. The wonderful thing about Mrs. Lynde's and Anne's relationship is that once they both made the hurdle past their first unfortunate encounter, they entered into community with each other simply because that is the way you "neighbor" in Avonlea. Mrs. Lynde and Anne honor the expectation that a neighbor is more than just someone with whom you live in close proximity. A neighbor in Avonlea is someone with whom, at the very least, you make an effort to get along.

Mrs. Lynde eventually comes to see that she was wrong in her assessment of Anne, just as Anne comes to see that there is good in Mrs. Lynde on the other side of her quick judgments. As the novel goes on, Mrs. Lynde becomes more loving just by being Anne's nearest neighbor. Anne, thanks to Marilla's insistence, is forced to make amends with Mrs. Lynde. And it is because of this openness to her neighbor that Anne ultimately discovers a kindred spirit in Mrs. Lynde.

Anne's indomitable opinion is that *everyone* is a possible kindred spirit. It is her constant curiosity of others that keeps her open and vulnerable, and ultimately, it's what allows her to love and be loved in return. But it is the community she chooses to embrace that sets the perfect stage for her flourishing.

HEROINE CHALLENGE

Take the Next Best Step

Wherever you are in your eating like a heroine journey, the next best step is the one right in front of you. Maybe hosting a dinner party isn't your thing. But what would the world look like if each of us ate one less meal alone per week? As we wrap our minds around the possibilities that come from eating like a heroine, think about the unique gifts you have to offer your community, and marvel along with Anne: "Isn't it splendid to think of all the things there are to find out about? It just makes me feel glad to be alive—it's such an interesting world."

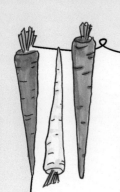

Recipe

Mrs. Barry's Humble Pie

"Mrs. Barry was here this afternoon, Anne. She wanted to see you, but I wouldn't wake you up. She says you saved Minnie May's life, and she is very sorry she acted as she did in that affair of the currant wine."

What exactly does Humble Pie taste like, we wonder?

Of course, it can't be any good: lukewarm, bitter, unsatisfying, probably. But what if, for our purposes here, we redeemed all those qualities and turned them into something cold, chocolatey, and decadent instead?

In that case, Humble Pie would taste exactly like Jenny's favorite no-bake chocolate pie: delicious on all accounts, for all parties, accused or groveling.

Ingredients

    4 oz. bittersweet chocolate chips

    1 C (2 sticks) salted butter, softened

    1 C white sugar or sucanat

    1 tsp. Pure Vanilla Extract

    4 whole eggs

    1 baked pie shell (Homemade or store-bought, no judgment either way. While Jenny and Lorilee differ strongly on Pie Crust Views, their friendship is stronger than a flaky flour and butter concoction.)

    Whipped cream for serving

1. In a small pot, melt the chocolate chips on low heat on the stove (you can also microwave them in a microwave safe bowl for about 4-5 minutes, until the chocolate is stirrable). Set aside to cool.

2. In a large bowl with an electric mixer, beat 1 cup (2 sticks) of salted butter and 1 cup of sugar until fluffy (about 1-2 minutes). When melted chocolate is cooled, drizzle it over the butter/sugar mixture. Add 1 teaspoon of vanilla extract. Beat the mixture thoroughly until combined (using the whisk attachment). Turn your mixer to a medium speed and over a period of about 15-20 minutes add in the eggs, one at a time, leaving about 5 minutes between each egg addition.

3. Once the pie filling is well mixed, pour it into the baked pie shell, scraping the bowl well. Smooth out the pie filling and place pie in the refrigerator to chill for at least two hours (although, longer is best).

4. Serve with a generous dollop of whipped cream on each slice.

ACKNOWLEDGMENTS

From Lorilee and Jenny

Many thanks to Victoria Duerstock for catching our vision for this book from the start. We love your momentum at End Game, and know you are always shooting for the stars, for us and all your authors.

To Hope Bolinger, for your cheerful and patient edits and for guiding us through a whopper of a citations list! We are grateful!

To our faithful agent Don Pape, who never gave up in finding a good home for our book baby, for cheering us on, and always being someone we could count on.

To Bunmi Ishola, for helping us amplify BIPOC heroines early on and for being a kindred spirit.

From Lorilee

To booksellers everywhere who share my dad's passion for placing the right book in the right hands at the right time. Keep up the good work!

To my darling Pastor Andrea Bult, for friendship, mutual Prince Edward Island love (can't believe you got to grow up there!), and for gamely eating cow tongue in what can only be described as a cheap book stunt. You are the best pastor ever and we adore you.

To Cynthia Beach for many years of writing and friendship, and for your enthusiasm and care.

To Sheri Rodriguez and Kim Sorrelle for laughs, love, and endless encouragement and support.

Thanks to my book club, Ann Byle, Erica Shier, Rachel Laughlin, Amy Diephouse, Tiffany Kreh, and Mary Franks, for all solidarity, encouragement, and for indulging me once a year on my Jane Austen fixation.

Thanks to The Guild, my writing sisterhood, Ann Byle again, Sharron Carrns, Alison Hodgson and Tracy Groot. Seriously, I would be a puddle of non-writing without you in my corner. Each of you has been a big fan of this book idea from day 1, and I treasure your heroic presence in my life over the last 18-23 years (depending on who you are!).

To my extended family, including my dear mother-in-law, Linda Craker, who is always keenly interested in discussions about how food was prepared in heroine days; and my sister-in-law, Jodi Connell, for support and for bringing us chicken soup when we had Covid! I hope both of you will love this book; I thought of you both many times while writing it.

To my beloved mom, Linda Reimer, who, at eighty-eight, is a heroine by anyone's standards. Every time I call you, you seem to be bustling in the kitchen, making Napolean Torte or borscht or something to serve to company. You emulate pinafore hospitality at its finest, with a touch of puffed sleeve panache. It is such a privilege to have you in my life at this point, praying for me and mine without ceasing, and loving us all so well. I love you more than you will ever know.

To my beautiful family, Doyle, Jonah, Ezra and Phoebe, and the sweetest daughter-in-law, Brenn. I love you all so, so much.

And finally, thank you endlessly and always, Jenny, for reaching out to me on Instagram several years ago to tell me you had read my Anne memoir. Since then, our friendship has turned into one of the most flourishing partnerships of my life, because that's what kindred spirits do—we make this old blue marble a brighter, kinder, place to live and love. I knew when you showed up at the Little House on the Prairie with the exact same Anne of Green Gables mask—on what turned out to be Carrie Ingalls' 150th birthday!—that you and I were meant to be forever friends. Thank you for all the laughter, creative collaboration, and bosom friend kismet. Writing the book and producing the podcast with you has been a delightful source of inspiration, delight, growth, and new horizons.

P.S. "Heyyy Almanzooo"

From Jenny

A big hug and many thanks to my loving family: Thank you to Eric, for your unwavering love, support, and belief in me. I don't deserve you. To Violet, Ivy, and Irvin for being just exactly who you are, and for the childlike joy you inadvertently contributed to this project. To my parents, Tim and Debbie, who have always been the first to encourage all of my dreams (even the very unreasonable and rather harebrained ones), and who set the tone for exploring creative ideas, and modeled generous hospitality, all throughout my childhood. I love you both dearly. To my weird and wonderful siblings who inspire me in so many ways, Stewart, Julie, and Sally, and to your beautiful families, thank you for your love and support. (With a special shout out to my dear sister-in-law Molly, for your insightful questions and cheerful encouragement throughout this whole process). Thank you to my wonderful mother-in-law, Linda, and to the memory of Jack. You both accepted and supported me from day one and have been a constant source of encouragement in all my creative endeavors. Thank you to my father-in-law Don, and Brenda, for all your love, support, and hospitality over the years. I love you all.

Thank you to the MAWS, my writing pals, Abby Anderson, Audra Yoder, and Kathleen Marsh, for your insights on an early draft of our proposal and your wildly gracious enthusiasm all along the way. (I don't need to tell you how much I *admire* each of you.) To my friends at Commonplace Books, for all your support and kindness and willingness to share my work over the years. To Fr. Yoder, for saying just the right thing when I needed some fear-of-failure counsel, and to all my church family: you model the true meaning of community and give me a place to truly be myself—I cannot imagine my life without you.

To Emily McCormick for your fiercely loyal friendship and for, in high school, informing me I would write a book one day. To Rachel Perteet for being my only L.M. Montgomery reading buddy for many, many years.

To Jennifer L. Scott and Anne Bogel for being some of the earliest supporters of my work, and whose belief in me had a profound impact. And to Keely Steger, thanks for being the best former assistant ever, but mostly for the timely GIFs.

To Amanda at the Lodge on Twinkle Lane for your generous hospitality toward a stranger, and your gift to my family at the perfect moment in this book-writing journey.

To Lorilee, where do I even begin? You embraced me with open arms (metaphorically at first, and eventually quite literally) after that first DM, and in addition to your friendship, you have been a gift from God in my life in so many ways—from being so generous with your writing wisdom to being such an example of gracious hospitality toward everyone you meet. No one is a stranger to you. Seeing how our weaknesses and strengths came together to create this book so seamlessly was a truly eye-opening experience, and one I will cherish forever. Your friendship has changed me, my abs are stronger from all the laughs, and I continue to learn so much from you. Love you, pal.

And last but certainly not least, my Kindred Spirit community and all my Carrot Top Paper Shop customers around the world—some of you have been with me since I began in 2015—words fail me in my gratitude toward you. Without you, I would not be able to do what I do and you would not be holding this book in your hands. Keep being the heroines that you are.

ENDNOTES

INTRODUCTION

Osborne, A. (2022). *The Emily Dickinson Cookbook: Recipes from Emily's Table Alongside the Poems that Inspire Them.* Harvard Common Press.

Hurston, Z. N. (2006). *Their Eyes Were Watching God.* HarperCollins.

The Florida Times-Union. (2010, December 23). *Maya Angelou puts thought into food as well as words.* Florida Times-Union. https://www.jacksonville.com/story/entertainment/books/2010/12/23/maya-angelou-puts-thought-food-well-words/15920799007/.

Walker, B. M. (1979). *The Little House Cookbook: Frontier Foods From Laura Ingalls Wilder.* HarperCollins.

"Dinner with Mr. Darcy: Recipes Inspired by the Novels and Letters of Jane Austen, by Pen Vogler—A Review." Austenprose. Last modified November 21, 2021. https://austenprose.com/2014/01/27/dinner-with-mr-darcy-recipes-inspired-by-the-novels-and-letters-of-jane-austen-by-pen-vogler-a-review/.

CHAPTER ONE

"Login • Instagram." Login • Instagram. Accessed January 9, 2024. https://www.instagram.com/revelry_picnics/. https://www.instagram.com/revelry_picnics/.

Coolidge, Susan. *What Katy Did.* 1908.

Ibid.

Hill, Kate. "How to Picnic Like the French." Saveur. Last modified October 23, 2019. https://www.saveur.com/french-picnic-how-to/.

Angelou, Maya. *I Know Why the Caged Bird Sings.* New York: Random House, 2010.

"Maya Angelou Know Better Do Better." Successful Spirit. Last modified February 8, 2023. https://www.thesuccessfulspirit.com/maya-angelou-know-better-do-better/.

"Emma: Picnicking on Box Hill." Jane Austen's World. Last modified April 26, 2009. https://janeaustensworld.com/2008/03/21/emma-picnicking-on-box-hill/.

Alcott, Louisa M. *Little Women (1868) Novel by: Louisa May Alcott*. Scotts Valley: Createspace Independent Publishing Platform, 2017.

Spyri, Johanna. *Heidi*. London: Puffin Books, 2014.

Montgomery, Lucy M. *Anne of Avonlea*. L. C. Page, 1909.

"Susanna Ives' Floating World." Susanna Ives' Floating World. Last modified April 21, 2021. https://susannaives.com/wordpress/2014/08/mrs-beeton-throws-a-ball-serves-a-wedding-breakfast-and-picnics-in-1866/.

Ryan, Pam M. *Esperanza Rising (Scholastic Gold)*. New York: Scholastic, 2012.

Cotler, Amy. *The Secret Garden Cookbook, Newly Revised Edition: Inspiring Recipes from the Magical World of Frances Hodgson Burnett's The Secret Garden*. Harvard Common Press, 2020.

Hanel, Marnie, Andrea Slonecker, and Jen Stevenson. *The Picnic: Recipes and Inspiration from Basket to Blanket*. Artisan Books, 2015.

Alcott, Louisa M. *Little Women (1868) Novel by: Louisa May Alcott*. Scotts Valley: Createspace Independent Publishing Platform, 2017.

Hgersh03. "Orzo with Roasted Vegetables." Food Network. Last modified July 22, 2015. https://www.foodnetwork.com/recipes/ina-garten/orzo-with-roasted-vegetables-recipe-1951921.

CHAPTER TWO

Taylor, Mildred D. *Roll of Thunder, Hear My Cry*. London: Penguin, 2004.

Ibid.

Pye, Mrs. J., and Julia A. Pye. *Invalid Cookery: A Manual of Recipes for the Preparation of Food for the Sick and Convalescent; to which is Added a Chapter of Practical Suggestions for the Sick-room*. 1880.

Harding, Kelli. *The Rabbit Effect: Live Longer, Happier, and Healthier with the Groundbreaking Science of Kindness*. Atria Books, 2020.

Porter, Eleanor H. *Pollyanna*. 1913.

Morell, Sally F., and Kaayla T. Daniel. *Nourishing Broth: An Old-Fashioned Remedy for the Modern World*. Grand Central Life & Style, 2014.

Bergstrom, Jenne, and Miko Osada. *The Little Women Cookbook: Novel Takes on Classic Recipes from Meg, Jo, Beth, Amy, and Friends.* Ulysses Press, 2019.

Austen, Jane. *Sense and Sensibility.* 1864.

Angelou, Maya. *Hallelujah! The Welcome Table: A Lifetime of Memories with Recipes.* London: Virago Press, 2006.

Beeton, Mrs. I. *The Book of Household Management.* Library of Alexandria, 1880.

Ryan, Pam M. *Esperanza Rising (Scholastic Gold).* New York: Scholastic, 2012.

CHAPTER THREE

Lovelace, Maud H. *Heaven to Betsy: A Betsy-Tacy High School Story.* Crowell, 1945.

Verner, Leslie. *Invited: The Power of Hospitality in an Age of Loneliness.* Harrisonburg: Herald Press, 2019.

Ibid.

Angelou, Maya. *I Know Why the Caged Bird Sings.* New York: Random House, 2010.

Coolidge.

Lovelace, Maud H. *Emily of Deep Valley: A Deep Valley Book.* New York: HarperCollins, 2011.

Conference Office. "The Meaning of Hospitality." Mosaic Mennonites. Last modified April 28, 2016. https://mosaicmennonites.org/2016/04/28/ the-meaning-of-hospitality/.

Perkins, Mitali. *Steeped in Stories: Timeless Children's Novels to Refresh Our Tired Soul: Timeless Children's Novels to Refresh Our Tired Souls.* Augsburg Fortress Publishers, 2021.

"Betsy, Tacy & Sunday Soup." Joëlle Anthony | Audio Book Narrator | Author | Mentor. Last modified August 4, 2023. https://joelleanthony.com/betsy-tacy-sunday-soup/.

Spyri, Johanna. *Heidi.* London: Puffin Books, 2014.

CHAPTER FOUR

Alcott.

Dinesen, Isak. *Babette's Feast.* New York: Random House, 2022.

"Maya Angelou Quote." A-Z Quotes. Accessed August 10, 2023. https://www.azquotes.com/quote/8570.

"A Way with Words and a Spice Rack (Published 2014)." The New York Times—Breaking News, US News, World News and Videos. Last modified June 2, 2014. https://www.nytimes.com/2014/06/04/dining/recalling-maya-angelous-love-of-cooking.html.

Burnett, Frances H. *A Little Princess*. London: Penguin UK, 2008.

Ibid.

https://www.zoranealehurston.com/resource/she-was-the-party-their-eyes-were-watching-god/.

CHAPTER FIVE

Angelou.

Austen, Jane. *Emma: 200th-Anniversary Annotated Edition (Penguin Classics Deluxe Edition)*. London: Penguin Classics, 2015.

Bergstrom, Jenne, and Miko Osada. *The Little Women Cookbook: Novel Takes on Classic Recipes from Meg, Jo, Beth, Amy, and Friends*. Ulysses Press, 2019.

Alcott.

"Sally Lunn Buns and Jane Austen Comfort Food." Delightful Repast. Last modified June 13, 2010. https://www.delightfulrepast.com/2010/06/sally-lunn-buns-and-jane-austen-comfort.html.

Bergstrom and Osada.

Vogler, Pen. *Tea with Jane Austen: Recipes inspired by her novels and letters*. CICO Books, 2016.

Martha Lloyd's Household Book: The Original Manuscript from Jane Austen's Kitchen. 2021.

Cotler.

Kolber, Aundi. *Strong Like Water: Finding the Freedom, Safety, and Compassion to Move Through Hard Things--And Experience True Flourishing*. Tyndale Refresh, 2023.

Burnett, Frances H. *The Secret Garden*. 1911.

Cotler.

Hurston.

Undset, Sigrid. Kristin Lavransdatter: (Penguin Classics Deluxe Edition). London: Penguin, 2005.

"Koselig is the New Hygge — A Philosophy for Dealing With Winter Blahs." Reader's Digest. Last modified January 12, 2023. https://www.rd.com/article/koselig/.

Allan, David G. "Why Are Norwegians So Happy? In a Word: 'koselig.'" CNN. Last modified July 1, 2019. https://www.cnn.com/2019/04/30/health/norway-koselig-hygge-cozy-nature-chasing-life-wisdom-project/index.html.

L'Engle, Madeleine. *A Wrinkle in Time.* London: Macmillan, 1962.

Angelou.

Aurell, Bronte. The Scandi Kitchen: Simple, delicious dishes for any occasion. Ryland Peters & Small, 2018.

Chapter Six

Garten, Ina. *Go-To Dinners: A Barefoot Contessa Cookbook.* Clarkson Potter, 2022.

Moranville, Wini, and Louisa M. Alcott. *The Little Women Cookbook: Tempting Recipes from the March Sisters and Their Friends and Family.* Harvard Common Press, 2019.

Harding, Kelli. *The Rabbit Effect: Live Longer, Happier, and Healthier with the Groundbreaking Science of Kindness.* Atria Books, 2020.

Capon, Robert F. *The Supper of the Lamb: A Culinary Reflection.* Eugene: Harvest, 1979.

De Cabo, Rafael, and Mark P. Mattson. "Effects of Intermittent Fasting on Health, Aging, and Disease."

New England Journal of Medicine 381, no. 26 (2019), 2541-2551. doi:10.1056/nejmra1905136.

Stephens, Gin. *Fast. Feast. Repeat.: The Comprehensive Guide to Delay, Don't Deny® Intermittent Fasting—Including the 28-Day FAST Start.* New York: St. Martin's Griffin, 2020.

Coolidge, Susan. *What Katy Did.* 1908.

Williams, Carolyn. "Top 5 Benefits of Meal Planning, According to An Expert." Personal Finance News—Yahoo Money. Last modified January 26, 2021. https://money.yahoo.com/top-5-benefits-meal-planning.

Priceonomics. "Here's How Much Money You Save By Cooking At Home." Forbes. Last modified July 10, 2018. https://www.forbes.com/sites/priceonomics/2018/07/10/heres-how-much-money-do-you-save-by-cooking-at-home/.

O'Dea, Stephanie. "Slow Cooker Take Out Fake Out Recipes." A Year of Slow Cooking. Last modified February 14, 2022. https://www.ayearofslowcooking.com/2016/06/slow-cooker-take-out-fake-out-recipes.html.

Cotler, Amy. *The Secret Garden Cookbook, Newly Revised Edition: Inspiring Recipes from the Magical World of Frances Hodgson Burnett's The Secret Garden.* Harvard Common Press, 2020.

Montgomery, L. M. *Rainbow Valley.* New York: Simon & Schuster, 2015.

Carman, Ronda. *The Art of Pantry Cooking: Meals for Family and Friends.* Rizzoli Publications, 2023.

CHAPTER SEVEN

Osborne, A. (2022). *The Emily Dickinson Cookbook: Recipes from Emily's Table Alongside the Poems that Inspire Them.* Harvard Common Press.

"Eat Like Jane Austen With Recipes From Her Sister-In-Law's Cookbook." Atlas Obscura. Last modified July 22, 2021. https://www.atlasobscura.com/articles/jane-austen-recipes-cookbook.

"Eat Like Jane Austen With Recipes From Her Sister-In-Law's Cookbook." Atlas Obscura. Last modified July 22, 2021. https://www.atlasobscura.com/articles/jane-austen-recipes-cookbook.

Ryan, Pam M. *Esperanza Rising.* New York: Scholastic, 2000. Taylor, Mildred D. *Roll of Thunder, Hear My Cry (Puffin Modern Classics).* London: Penguin, 2004.

Osborne, A. (2022). *The Emily Dickinson Cookbook: Recipes from Emily's Table Alongside the Poems that Inspire Them.* Harvard Common Press.

Ibid.

Ibid.

Wilder, Laura I. *Little House in the Big Woods.* New York: HarperCollins, 2004.

Austen, Jane. *Pride and Prejudice.* 1918.

Angelou, Maya. *I Know Why the Caged Bird Sings.* New York: Random House, 2010.

"Wilder Wednesday—Venison." Hen Scratches. Last modified May 26, 2015. https://henscratches.wordpress.com/2015/05/27/wilder-wednesday-venison/.

CHAPTER EIGHT

Smith, Betty. *A Tree Grows in Brooklyn.* New York: Random House, 1992.

Alcott, Louisa M. *Little Women (1868) Novel by: Louisa May Alcott.* Scotts Valley: Createspace Independent Publishing Platform, 2017.

Montgomery, L. M. *Anne of Windy Poplars.* Tundra Books, 2014.

Austen, Jane. *Persuasion: (Penguin Classics Deluxe Edition)*. London: Penguin, 2011.

Angelou, Maya. *I Know Why the Caged Bird Sings*. New York: Random House, 2010.

Taylor, Mildred D. *Roll of Thunder, Hear My Cry*. London: Penguin, 2004.

Wilder, Laura I. *Little House on the Prairie*. New York: HarperCollins, 2004.

Bronte, Charlotte. *Jane Eyre*. London: Penguin UK, 2010.

Taylor, Sydney. *All-of-a-Kind Family*. Follettbound, 2002.

Smith, Betty. *A Tree Grows in Brooklyn*. New York: Random House, 1992.

Coolidge, Susan. *What Katy Did*. 1908.

Alvarez, Julia. *In the Time of the Butterflies*. Chapel Hill: Algonquin Books, 2010.

Nast, Condé. "Moors and Christians (Moros Y Cristianos)." Epicurious. Last modified October 30, 2013. https://www.epicurious.com/recipes/food/views/moors-and-christians-em-moros-y-cristianos-em-51203610.

McCauley, Marcie. "The Betsy-Tacy Books by Maud Hart Lovelace: An Appreciation." Literary Ladies Guide. Last modified August 28, 2022. https://www.literaryladiesguide.com/literary-musings/the-betsy-tacy-books-by-maud-hart-lovelace-an-appreciation/.

Lovelace, Maud H. *Betsy-Tacy*. New York: HarperCollins, 2011.

"Rilla of Ingleside, by Lucy Maud Montgomery." Book Reviews from a Christian Worldview at Reading to Know. Accessed August 16, 2023. https://www.readingtoknow.com/2011/01/rilla-of-ingleside-by-lucy-maud.html.

Osborne, A. (2022). *The Emily Dickinson Cookbook: Recipes from Emily's Table Alongside the Poems that Inspire Them*. Harvard Common Press.

Wilder, Laura I. *Little Town on the Prairie*. New York: HarperCollins, 2007.

Austen, Jane. *Sense and Sensibility*. 1864.

CHAPTER NINE

"Culture on My Mind—Every Storm Runs Out Of Rain." Creative Criticality. Last modified February 14, 2020. https://creativecriticality.net/2020/02/14/culture-on-my-mind-every-storm-runs-out-of-rain/.

Bergstrom, Jenne, and Miko Osada. *The Little Women Cookbook: Novel Takes on Classic Recipes from Meg, Jo, Beth, Amy, and Friends*. Ulysses Press, 2019.

Alcott, Louisa M. *Little Women (1868) Novel by: Louisa May Alcott*. Scotts Valley: Createspace Independent Publishing Platform, 2017.

Nast, Condé. "21 Pomegranate Recipes: The Fruit Equivalent of Gushers." Bon Appétit. Last modified December 9, 2015. https://www.bonappetit.com/recipes/slideshow/pomegranate-salad-chicken-recipes.

Vogler, Pen. *Tea with Jane Austen: Recipes inspired by her novels and letters.* CICO Books, 2016.

Olsen, Kirstin. *Cooking with Jane Austen.* Santa Barbara: Greenwood Publishing Group, 2005.

Sheehan, Jessie. *The Vintage Baker: More Than 50 Recipes from Butterscotch Pecan Curls to Sour Cream Jumbles.* San Francisco: Chronicle Books, 2018.

Montgomery, L. M. *Anne of Ingleside.* Tundra Books, 2014.

Montgomery, L. M. *Anne of Windy Poplars.* Tundra Books, 2014.

Montgomery, L. M. *Anne of Ingleside.* Tundra Books, 2014.

Burnett, Frances H. *A Little Princess.* New York: Simon & Schuster, 2022. Accessed August 18, 2023. chrome-extension://efaidnbmnnnibpcajpcglclefindmkaj/https://ag.umass.edu/sites/ag.umass.edu/files/fact-sheets/pdf/currants.pdf.

Nast, Condé. "If You're Rolling Dough, You Need a Roul'pat." Bon Appétit. Last modified December 21, 2020. https://www.bonappetit.com/story/roulpat.

"Chestnut Recipes." BBC Good Food | Recipes and Cooking Tips - BBC Good Food. Accessed August 18, 2023. https://www.bbcgoodfood.com/recipes/collection/chestnut-recipes.

"Philopena—Definition, Examples, Related Words and More at Wordnik." Wordnik.com. Accessed August 18, 2023. https://www.wordnik.com/words/philopena.

Lovelace, Maud H. *Emily of Deep Valley: A Deep Valley Book.* New York: HarperCollins, 2011.

"What the Hell Was Shrimp Wiggle?" The Takeout. Last modified October 23, 2019. https://thetakeout.com/what-is-shrimp-wiggle-joy-of-cooking-1839236691.

CHAPTER TEN

Jun, Tasha. *Tell Me the Dream Again: Reflections on Family, Ethnicity, and the Sacred Work of Belonging.* Carol Stream: Tyndale House Publishers, 2023.

Ryan, Pam M. *Esperanza Rising (Scholastic Gold).* New York: Scholastic, 2012.

"The Nose, an Emotional Time Machine (Published 2008)." The New York Times—Breaking News, US News, World News and Videos. Last modified August 7, 2008. https://www.nytimes.com/2008/08/05/science/05angier.html.

Craker, Lorilee. *Anne of Green Gables, My Daughter, & Me: What My Favorite Book Taught Me about Grace, Belonging & the Orphan in Us All.* Carol Stream: Tyndale House Publishers, 2015.

Hurston, Z. N. (2006). *Their Eyes Were Watching God.* HarperCollins.

Opie, Frederick D. *Zora Neale Hurston on Florida Food: Recipes, Remedies and Simple Pleasures.* History Press, 2015.

"The Food of Zora Neale Hurston." KCRW. Accessed August 18, 2023. https://www.kcrw.com/culture/shows/good-food/migas-las-street-food-conundrum-savethecremeegg/the-food-of-zora-neale-hurston.

Schulz, Kathryn. "Eat Your Words: Anthony Bourdain on Being Wrong." Slate Magazine. Accessed August 18, 2023. https://slate.com/news-and-politics/2010/06/eat-your-words-anthony-bourdain-on-being-wrong.html.

Tan, Amy. *The Joy Luck Club: A Novel.* London: Penguin, 2006.

Taylor, Mildred D. *Roll of Thunder, Hear My Cry.* London: Penguin, 2004.

Montgomery, L. M. *Rainbow Valley.* Tundra Books, 2014.

Lovelace, Maud H. *Emily of Deep Valley: A Deep Valley Book.* New York: HarperCollins, 2011.

"Your Mother Died. Now She Wants to Tell You Her Secrets. (Published 2022)." The New York Times—Breaking News, US News, World News and Videos. Last modified February 2, 2022. https://www.nytimes.com/2022/02/01/books/group-text-black-cake-charmaine-wilkerson.html.

CHAPTER ELEVEN

Ephron, Nora. *I Remember Nothing: And Other Reflections.* New York: Vintage, 2011.

"Captcha Challenge…." Captcha Challenge….Accessed August 18, 2023. https://quizlet.com/570256029/stomach-flash-cards/.

"What's Making Anne of Green Gables Turn Green in the Latest Google Doodle?" Gizmodo. Last modified November 30, 2015. https://gizmodo.com/whats-making-anne-of-green-gables-turn-green-in-the-lat-1745202785.

Ephron, Nora. *I Remember Nothing: And Other Reflections.* New York: Vintage, 2011.

Angelou, Maya. *Letter To My Daughter.* London: Hachette UK, 2010.

We can't wait to meet you at the table as together,
we listen and learn from our bookish favorites,
how to eat like a heroine.